by Robert Street

ISBN N°: 0 948204 59 1

Published by: Barny Books, Hough-on-the-Hill, Grantham, Lincolnshire

Produced by: **TUCANN***design&print*
19 High Street, Heighington, Lincoln LN4 1RG • Tel & Fax: 01522 790009

··· **Chapter 1** ···

My mother, Ivy, was the bread winner in our family. She bought and sold second hand furniture, paintings, anything that she could sell in her shop.

She had married my father in 1917, soon after he had been invalided out of the First World War. He had been shot in the throat at Gallipoli. His vocal chords had been damaged and he spoke with a hoarse, gravelly voice. He'd been in the regular army. He had no trade or profession to fall back on and was only able to do casual work and there wasn't much of that about, not between the wars. He even had to sell his medals and his treasured collections of butterflies from his army days in India to buy food for the family.

We lived in Cheltenham when I was small, Montpelier Villas. My mother woke me early one morning and said that we had to catch the train to Birmingham. My father would follow later with the furniture. We always seemed to be moving around. My mother would set up a business only to move on again when it failed or trade was so poor there was no point in carrying on. We had relatives in Birmingham and that's why we went there. Mother rented a shop in Hall Green at first, but trade was no better there than it had been in Cheltenham so we moved to Sparkbrook, Gladstone Road. I liked it there. There was a lot of poverty, but there was a general honesty and feeling of community. Mother's business did better here and our standard of living wasn't too bad, but we did have some bad times and were only too pleased to visit relations for Sunday lunch.

In the summer holidays I would go to visit my Uncle George with my brother Eddie, our cousins and some friends. He was a builder. We would help make the concrete blocks for the new houses he was building. Each day we would travel a couple of miles to the building site in Wake Green Road, make blocks, riddle sand, or undertake some other menial task, all for a few sandwiches and threepence a day. But it was worth it, we had the time of our lives.

Mother's business carried on much the same, opening and closing shops and us moving from house to house. We settled at Anderton Road then moved round the corner to Palmerston Road but mother managed to keep the house at Anderton Road and let it out to lodgers. That was her finest business venture. We had lodgers in both houses and my father did the odd jobs and collected the rent, while mother carried on with her furniture business. Eventually we took on seven more houses.

This was a happy time for me, I was fourteen and had left school. I had started working at a bakers.

However, things weren't all good, the depression was still persisting leaving many people poverty stricken. Most of the working class people lived virtually on the breadline. Poverty goes hand in hand with poor health and in the poorer communities diseases such as tuberculosis and rickets were common. In 1934 I contracted scarlet fever and spent weeks isolated in an attic room, cut off from all outside contact with the exception of my mother and father. Even my brother was not allowed to see me. In the evening my father used to sit with me armed with his bottle of beer, light a cigarette and tell me about his days in the Army. I used to say, "Tell me about India Dad", or "Tell me about the war Dad". Little did I think that ten years later I would go to parts of India where he had been. It was at these times that I think I got closest to my father, with him telling me of his Battalion, The Fourth Worcesters and landing on W Beach at Gallipoli.

They were following the First Lancaster Fusiliers Battalion that had run into a strong contingent of Turkish troops defending positions on the cliffs. My father's recollection of the First World War and the suffering and horror he witnessed made me appreciate some of the reasons which led him to drink to escape that reality. He was in the 29th British Division of the Fourth Battalion of the Worcestershire Regiment. He was a regular member of the Army since 1911, not one of the people swept with the emotion of patriotism. This was his job and he was called into action to fight in the Dardanelles in 1915.

The Fourth Worcesters landed on W Beach to be met by a hail of bullets, cutting the young soldiers down in vast numbers as they moved up the beach to the cliffside path. My father recalled talking to a young officer of the Lancashire Regiment, clinging to the cliffside, only to find that he was stone dead. Eventually, the Worcestershire Battalion got to the top of the cliffs and advanced several miles inland, settling down and digging in to establish their position.

My father's duty was to man the Vickers machine gun. As the darkness drew in, he sited the gun to hit any attacking enemy in the lower part of the body. During the night when noises were heard in no-man's land, my father was instructed to pan machine gun fire into the darkness and this was met by screams and moans. In the light of the day, he witnessed large groups of dead and wounded, many with limbs hanging off where the bullets from his machine gun had cut the Turkish soldiers down. My father and his comrades did what they could for the wounded Turks, putting their packs under their wounded legs to support them, giving them water and tending to their wounds as best they could. This was far better than the treatment some of the Turks gave our wounded British soldiers. They were more likely to torture them to death, leaving them nailed to wooden crosses.

Some weeks later, my father was in action again. He opened fire with his machine gun. A Turkish sniper's bullet hit his machine gun's water cooling casing around the barrel which he plugged to stop leaking water and opened fire once again at his target. Another bullet thudded into the path alongside him and again he focused on his target. Suddenly, a blow like a sledgehammer hit him in the throat, knocking him over backwards. The sniper's bullet had caught him across the throat ripping it open, severing his windpipe causing him to choke on the blood from his own wound. The bullet had also damaged the vocal chords so his cries could not be heard. His comrades roughly bandaged his throat and dragged him away from the machine gun nest.

He had a choice to stay there and bleed to death or attempt to make his way to the first aid dressing station. He picked bits of shattered bone-like tissue from his throat to breathe better, feeling cold through shock and loss of blood. He unstrapped an unused thick folded great-coat from a nearby dead Turk's body, put it on and crawled back to the front line dressing station, waiting to be dealt with. There was a constant barrage of shell fire exploding around the area of the dressing station and suddenly my father felt as if he was sitting in water, only to find there was a stream of blood flowing beneath him.

He decided to move to another dressing station further back from the front line. He had heard that one of the Commanding Officers was going round shooting those soldiers severely injured, to put them out of their misery. Mercy killing they called it. So he kept going and eventually arrived at the troop ship, the 'River Clyde'. It was here that the medics performed an operation. There was no anaesthetic. They tried to fit tubes into his damaged windpipe. He had to be awake in order that they could ascertain whether or not the operation was allowing him to breathe satisfactorily. The wound was left gaping to heal on its own and he was sent to a hospital in the Middle East for convalescence. That was the end of his military service and at the age of twenty four his Army career was over. He was discharged to spend the rest of the war testing machine guns in England, later to be fully discharged with a War Pension of one pound per week.

His stories were not all about fighting. He talked about life in different lands and adventures he had experienced. I never forgot them. The four of us were all working, but money was still tight. I was getting twelve shillings a week working from eight until six o'clock in the evening. Then war was declared. I tried to join up straight away but was told to return when I was older.

In 1940 things accelerated somewhat. My brother, cousins and close friends had all been called up. In the months ahead a friend was killed in the battle at Dunkirk and another held as a prisoner of war. We soon realised after Dunkirk, that the war effort was not going well. One night while I listened to the radio, there was an appeal for local defence volunteers to protect our District from German paratroopers, inviting men from sixteen to sixty five to join at local police stations. I decided to join immediately and enrolled at Sparkhill Police Station. While I was getting ready, there was a knock at the door. My mate Jackie Waring had got the same idea. I had known Jackie from our school days; he was one of the original crowd who used to come on the cycling and fishing trips we had as kids. Anyway, we enrolled and were led through to a room at the rear of the police station to meet a mixed crowd of men, young and old, being shown how to use an old Lee Enfield rifle, loading and unloading dummy ammunition.

The next night we reported to Taunton Road Barracks where we were put into patrols, given a steel helmet and an armband with LDV (Local Defence Volunteers), on it. Later we were handed a clip of five 303 bullets and a pick axe handle for our first dusk to dawn patrol on some playing fields near Moseley Grammar School on the Wake Green Road, using the tower of the main school building for a lookout post and to plot fires, telephoning the appropriate authority to deal with them. An ex-First World War NCO, whom we nicknamed 'Old Bill', due to his likeness to some First World War cartoon character, had the only 303 Enfield rifle in the patrol. He was the senior and in charge. He was a right character. He had an awful habit of hiding in hedges and bushes and suddenly jumping out in the pitch blackness of the night shouting, 'Who goes there?' to some poor unsuspecting person. The panic stricken people would give their identity, whilst he held his bayonet inches from their throat and, when satisfied, would remove the bayonet saying, 'Pass friend', in his strong Brummie accent, at the same time blowing his beery breath over them. He kept us all on our toes and we would be extra vigilant if someone told us 'Old Bill' was on duty. We were told that in the event of an attack, should he get killed or wounded, we would grab his rifle using our own 303 bullets to continue the fight. Until then, the pick axe handles were to be our only defence against any Nazi paratroopers.

We undertook our dawn to dusk patrols several nights per week. Within a month we had rifles and fifty rounds of ammunition each. We had bayonet training and rifle practice. By the time I left to join the army we were properly armed, even having machine guns and grenades.

Whilst patrolling by Moseley Grammar school one night during an air raid, we noticed a light flashing from a nearby tree, obviously an enemy agent. We went after him but some idiot shouted and that gave the game away. He jumped from the tree, got on a motorbike and disappeared. During another raid, someone in the tower saw a flare being launched from behind one of the big houses further down the Wake Green Road. It was to guide the German bombers onto their targets. Our sports field patrol rushed directly over to search the empty house, but whoever it was had gone. It was also said that a spy had infiltrated our Homeguard. Apparently this thick set, beer swilling newcomer did not fool the Ex First World War guys. He had appeared on the scene, with no satisfactory background or history. He was a young man about twenty, well educated, but although I didn't notice, there was a telltale sign in his accent that the old soldiers recognised. The police took him away after a week.

By now, the war effort was mobilising quickly but soon the horrors of war were to strike as the Germans carried out bombing raids. Their primary target in the city was the BSA ammunitions factory in Small Heath, just around the corner from where we lived.

Our first experience of air raids was during September and October 1940 when we saw hundreds of lights in the distant skyline, enemy aircraft dropping flares to light up the area. Exploding distant bombs lit the city beneath as fires raged. At first we patrolled near Swanshurst Park, Moseley, around the anti aircraft guns which thundered a barrage of flak at the enemy aircraft as they flew over the city. Suddenly though, showers of hot metal, shrapnel from our own flak fell from the sky, forcing us to take shelter.

At home, the situation was different. The government provided air raid shelters, Anderson shelters. These were constructed of corrugated iron on an iron angle frame and were simply left outside peoples' houses for them to assemble. Everybody mucked in, helping the old, less fortunate and those who lived alone or could not cope. The idea was to position the shelter down the garden, away from the house, with the base four feet underground, so that people could get below ground during air raids. We had one of these shelters in our garden, but found it too cold in the winter, so we stayed indoors, sitting on the cellar steps.

Photograph courtesy of Birmingham Post and Mail Ltd

My father wasn't too bothered about the raids and would stay in the house or even go out. On one occasion, there was a near miss. A bomb had gone off about thirty yards away, blowing out our windows and front door. We were immediately concerned for Dad and could not find him anywhere. He finally turned up with a bottle of beer, as if nothing had happened.

Home Guard duties still continued and further training was given. On one occasion, I arrived at Taunton Road Drill Hall about a quarter to eight. It was October 1940 and a first aid lecture was to be given by a doctor. Looking at the Carlton Picture House opposite, I almost decided to give it a miss and see a film called 'Typhoon', about the South Seas. I had been waiting for this particular film to come round for sometime. Fortunately I put duty before pleasure and went into the Drill Hall and up the stairs to the lecture room. The blackouts were drawn covering the windows and a single electric light bulb lit our room. About twenty of us took seats and the doctor began his lecture.

As he talked the sirens started to wail. The doctor carried on talking, showing us how to dress wounds and asked us if we wished him to continue. Of course, we said yes.

The bombs were dropping in the distance and getting nearer. We all felt scared, but no one wanted to speak out or be the first to say 'Lets take cover'. So we stuck it out. Suddenly the blackouts to the window were blown into the room on top of us. The light went out and the room rocked, filling up with dust and smoke as we were thrown on the floor by the power of the blast. The building stayed put and after a few seconds we collected ourselves and looked with amazement through the shattered windows. All the lights came on in the picture house opposite. The manager had put the lights on to help the wounded people out of their seats. A bomb had gone off in front of the screen.

Earlier the manager had cleared the front rows of the seats of all but a few people when the raid had started, moving most of them under the balcony, for greater safety. Still people were killed or wounded in their seats. During the few minutes the lights were on, the wounded were mobilised and taken from the wrecked cinema. The dead were to be moved after the raid had finished.

Someone shouted to put the lights out. We were organised by the doctor to tend to the injured. A wounded usherette had been blown onto the road and was moaning. The doctor ordered us to carry her on a door that was lying on the pavement and take her to the barracks. We walked round a large crater from a second bomb that had fallen in the middle of the road.

The cinema itself was terrible. There was a crowd of wounded people, some sitting, others laying on the floor. A girl lay near the door crying for her mother. Another person started taking names and addresses. The doctor and other men bandaged some of the wounded. A middle aged man sat near the injured girl, with a hole the size of a penny in his forehead. He seemed to be quite normal in speech and talked quite coherently.

We were then called away to search the seats inside the picture house, for any wounded that had been missed. The main part of the picture house was wrecked, the seats covered in dust. Rubble was lying everywhere. We moved about through half light as most of the front part of the roof had been blown away.

We noticed a figure in the seats. The NCO moved over and shone the torch on a woman with her hands clasped together sitting quite comfortably as one would to watch a film. She had no head, just a dust covered stump of a neck. It was horrific. Near the front a young lad about twelve was dead between the seats. The NCO checked him for life but, there wasn't any. He was dead, curled up as if asleep. We found two more people, a man and a woman, bus driver and conductress. There were no marks on them. They too were in their seats as if they were asleep, both killed by the blast. We searched the rubble before leaving the job for the others the next day. Moving back to the foyer, we saw the man with the hole in his forehead had died, as had the girl lying by the door.

Returning to the barracks we were told to go to the canteen for a drink and some food; however, our first horror of the war had taken away our appetites. Even the beer tasted flat, but we drank it anyway. After leaving the barracks we were told to man one end of the road and prevent anyone coming through the emergency services. Four of us from the Homeguard were detailed. A man tried to enter, but we halted him telling him that the road was closed and we were ordered not to let anyone through. He became anxious and angry but soon calmed down when he found two bayonets pushed hard against his throat. One of the older NCO's came across, to calm the situation down and the man left, hurling abuse as he walked away.

Around one o'clock in the morning several vans came to collect the dead and at four o'clock we were relieved of our duty and sent home to get some sleep. My parents were glad to see me as they had heard about the bombing but had no news of me or Jackie. The horror that we had seen had left us numb to their concern, the sickening sights left me unable to eat properly for several days.

We then walked round to Jackie's road and found many of the houses ablaze. Jackie checked to see if his family were alright. They were relieved he was safe too. I had seen enough for one evening and made my way home.

As winter passed and spring of 1941 approached, the fear of invasion passed and our own guard duties were cut to two nights a week. I was twenty one years old and working as a tool setter, a reserved occupation. I felt that it was time to join up, but failed the army medical. I had to return to my boring job.

The air raids didn't stop. Incendiary bombs set buildings ablaze, lighting up the city skyline and guiding more German bombers onto their targets. One night the fires were so bad, the brickwork to one building glowed red with the heat. When the firefighters sprayed water on it the colour changed to black, only to turn red again when the hose was moved to another area of the fire. The days after the raids were spent trying to regain some semblance of order. I remember seeing a factory operating with a large area of the roof missing. A bomb had done the damage earlier, blowing a big machine over. It was righted and business continued as usual.

I took a Monday off in March 1942 and went down to the recruiting office to try and join the Army yet again for the third time. The first time I was rejected for being too young, then for being medically unfit, slightly deaf in one ear and an injured back. This time I was turned down for being in a reserved occupation. The recruiting sergeant told me what an important job I was doing to help the war effort, but this was no compensation. I felt I needed to join the Army to achieve something with my life. I explained to him that I was keen to join because of the family history of regular soldiering. Eventually he said that if I was prepared to join the Army for seven years, with five years on reserve service, they would take me. I thought quickly and replied 'yes', and was sent through to the medical centre for further adjudication. When the medic got to the hearing test and whispered in my ear, I gave a standard answer, knowing what the answer was from the last time. I asked to join the Worcestershire Regiment, my father's regiment in the First World War. I was in. The next day I told my friend Jackie Waring that I had joined up and he did the same, even joining the same regiment.

I thought my parents would be pleased but they weren't. My father knew from his own experience what could happen in wartime.

We gave our notice and left our jobs. We handed in our uniforms to the Homeguard Stores and found that we had a few weeks to kill prior to reporting for duty. My mother asked if she could see me off, but not wanting to see her upset, I preferred to say my goodbyes at home and be waved off from New Street station by our girlfriends.

We went to Norton Barracks until July 1942.

After one period of leave, my friend Jackie, did not return to the barracks. Apparently there was some domestic trouble at home. However I returned as usual. When he was noticed absent at roll call the sergeant sent for me. I explained what I knew and was given another pass the following weekend to bring him back, or tell him that he may risk being put on charge for desertion. Anyway, when I arrived home, Jackie's problems seemed to have blown over, well almost, and I persuaded him to come back to the barracks with me. He was lucky, the sergeant was fairly lenient on him and he only got spud bashing, or 'jankers' as we used to call it, and a week's loss of pay. Obviously he wasn't pleased, but this was preferable to spending time in the glasshouse.

We had our passing out parade and were posted to Market Rasen, Lincolnshire - too far away for weekend leave in Birmingham.

It was now September 1942 and our army training became more intense, more PT, marching, assault course training, parading, drilling and so on, to get us fit and polish up on our army disciplines. It was at this time a black haired, quiet, well spoken lad joined our ranks; his name was John Harman. He was not only young but very knowledgeable. It was his courage which was to make him famous later, for he won the Victoria Cross and may well have altered the course of the battle at Kohima.

Another one of the chaps at Market Rasen was called Barton. He was always in trouble for being too outspoken, but he was a great sportsman. The Sergeant Major wanted him to remain on the staff at the camp to play in the camp's football team, but Barton wanted to be drafted with his mates. The Sergeant Major explained that he could stay at the camp, be promoted to an NCO and need not go to war. Barton would not hear of this and said that he wanted to go with his friends on draft, abroad. As our lorry moved off Barton was last on board and the Sergeant Major stood in the middle of the road and shouted, 'I shall be saluting your memorial, you silly sod'. Barton swore quietly as he got on. Unfortunately, the Sergeant Major was right, for two years later Barton was killed in action on the Burma front line - just to be with his mates.

We seemed to be undertaking endless route marches. Marching with a full pack and weapons for up to thirty miles a day, and the same the next day. Neat lines of soldiers as far as you could see, marching through lovely, unspoilt countryside. This of course, was strange to some of us, used to life in the inner city. We were living and working in the country and passed down beautiful lanes with fruit laden trees and wild raspberries growing alongside, not in the shop window or market as at home. Sometimes to break up the monotony of the march we would sing popular songs of the day.

One march was to Scarborough, one hundred miles away, again with full pack. A thousand men took part and marched all day with only ten minutes rest each hour. Not only this, but we had to take turns to carry heavy weapons such as the Bren gun. I prayed that I would get my turn early on in the march, as I couldn't imagine being able to carry it towards the end. At the end of each day we would set up camp at a nearby farm and nurse our blisters. Meals were prepared in a field kitchen and sanitary accommodation dug in a field close by. I was physically sick at the end of each day with exhaustion and would rush to the toilet where one would have to squat precariously over two wooden poles, taking care not to slip and fall into the stinking mess below. The sight itself was enough to put you off; I didn't linger there too long if I could help it. The camps were usually in the middle of nowhere, with us roughing it, perhaps sleeping on straw or hay in some old barn or outbuilding, making the best of it to get what sleep we could.

I had leave over Christmas and on the 14th January 1943 we were packed into a troop train bound for Liverpool and there we boarded the 'Mootan'.

We were allocated our section of the mess deck. Hooks on beams were provided on which to sling our hammocks. These were rolled up during the day, giving us some room to sit down at a long wooden table for meals. The ship was packed with troops. Then the ship moved out but it didn't move very far. It moved out into the middle of the Mersey and there we stayed. We could see the large buildings of Liverpool. One of the men came from Liverpool but he could only do the same as us, stand on deck and stare.

Then in the night the ship started to move again and we joined the rest of the convoy at Greenock.

We were detailed to carry life jackets at all times. We used them for pillows at night. We were also given a canvas bag containing a tin of survival chocolate which was tied to our packs, but a lot of us had ours stolen by men who would sneak up behind us and cut the string. We weren't worried. We were convinced that we wouldn't need it. We knew that we could deal with any U boats that put in an appearance.

The sea in January was very rough and most of the soldiers were sea-sick. The floor of our mess deck toilets was awash with seawater and vomit. The smell was so bad that some of us used to go on deck to be sick, although we were warned not to in case we fell overboard in the rough weather. I was too ill to climb into my hammock and lay on the floor under the table.

As we neared Gibraltar, the weather improved and we were ordered to wear our tropical kit. The convoy separated, half going in to the Mediterranean. We went south. As we reached the African coast, we saw sights we had never dreamed about, flying fish playing in the ship's wake and dolphins swimming and diving alongside us. At Freetown, the ship was surrounded by small boats laden with fruit, nuts and anything else they wanted to sell. We'd never seen anything like it. We weren't allowed to buy anything for fear of disease, so just stood and stared in amazement. We went on to Durban and had five days there. We set sail, escorted by destroyers. A lady in white sang to us as we left port. She sang to all the convoys that set sail from there. I think it was to boost morale. She had a lovely voice and we often talked about her.

In February we arrived at Bombay. It smelt foul and the heat was almost unbearable. We had a few hours to look round before we boarded the train. I'd never seen scenes like it in my life. There were snake charmers, beggars, knife throwers, street magicians who crowded round us in the hope of getting a few coppers. It was difficult to take it all in. The pavements seemed to be stained with blood, but we discovered that it was the residue of betel nuts which the Indians chewed and spat out. There was poverty and squalor all around and we were accosted by street traders, pimps and all sorts.

··· Chapter 2 ···

Although my father had described the country in such detail, nothing could have prepared me for the sights and sounds of India. It was a relief to leave Bombay and board the train for Allahabad.

The old steam train on which we were to travel, was not the old Pullman English style as we expected, but more like those used in the American wild west films, with steps up to the back of the carriages and even an American style cow catcher on the front. The carriages were split up into compartments to hold six men, three on each side and that was where we slept or sat during the journey. Some of the other carriages had open areas to eat meals or drink tea, made by those who were on cookhouse duty. This involved one of us going up to the driver of the train whenever it stopped and getting hot water from the train's boiler, which came down through a particular water pipe from which we filled our bucket. A soldier would jab a couple of holes in a tin of carnation milk with his bayonet and throw in a handful of sugar, stirring it all with the bayonet and the bucket of tea would be shared around. There would be fruit and charwallahs on stations where the train stopped, that sold fruit and tea in clay cups. One of the Anglo-Indians with us would call the fruitwallah who would appear with a basket, laden with all types of fruit and nuts. These Anglo-Indians would help us haggle with the fruitwallah and we would finally agree a price.

The stations themselves were a fantastic sight. They were full of all sorts of people. The train service was never on a regular basis and people could be at the station for several days waiting for their train. When it was due the station guard would strike a piece of old railway track that was hanging by some rope, tied to one of the wooden beams of the station building. Hordes of people would appear, from everywhere. It was like a scene from the Bible as they swept towards the train, dressed in their white flowing garments. When they tried to board the train itself, all hell let loose. We were alright though, as we were in the part of the train reserved for British troops. The locals would run up to the train, throw their luggage on, only to see it thrown off by somebody else. It was farcical, but they all seemed to get on, hanging on the sides, roof, or anywhere else they could grab.

We stored our rifles under long wooden seats which lifted up and then would sit or sleep on top so no-one could steal them. We had heard that Lee Enfield British rifles could be sold for up to one hundred pounds on the north-west frontier of India. Therefore, not only were we sleeping or sitting on top of our weapons, all doors were guarded by armed soldiers, twenty-four hours a day and especially when the train stopped. As we travelled across the open country it appeared as if we were going back in time, the culture, the buildings, it couldn't have been more different to Birmingham. This feeling increased when we stopped at an isolated station and an armed Indian Police escort led a line of chained Dacoits, wild looking men, who had committed some crime or other.

Eventually we arrived at Allahabad Barracks, modern brick built blocks with sports fields, plunge baths and all mod cons. Native servants were provided to keep us clean and smart and they would lay our uniforms on our beds and attend to all our laundry and domestic duties. Another servant arrived at five o'clock in the morning and shaved us while we were asleep under our mosquito nets in the long barrack room. We slept in a charpye, an Indian style bedstead with rope weaving in place of springs and three coconut fibre cushions instead of a mattress. Four bamboo poles supported our mosquito nets at night. The rifle racks were screwed and bolted down in the centre of the room, the weapons secured with a long steel flat bar, chained and padlocked to prevent theft by locals. It was not unusual for us to stand to during the night as volatile religious factions clashed nearby.

It all seemed ideal, safe, sound and healthy, but it was not. As the weather got hotter and hotter and the rains of the monsoon beckoned, the heat was almost beyond belief. Dampened bamboo matts hung in the doorways of our huts, to try to keep them cool, but didn't have much effect. Our corporal at Allahabad was a good chap, but a bit too easy going really. Marching in the hot sun one day, in a very unsoldierly manner, our strict regimental Sergeant Major halted us, gave us a good dressing down and had us and the corporal double march the rest of the way to the cookhouse. We were all soaked with sweat although it was only a short distance. We were lucky, he could have made it a lot worse. The heat was so intense there, even walking home was an effort. One day a squaddie broke ranks and walked in a tight circle before he fell on the floor with heat stroke; he was taken away to sick bay. As the year went on the months got hotter and hotter, many of the beds became empty in our barrack room and were put up against the barrack wall; their occupiers away in hospital with heat stroke or one of the other tropical diseases such as malaria, dysentery or smallpox, thinning perhaps twenty percent of our numbers.

The authorities decided that the Battalion was to be given ten days in the cool clean air of a mountain hill station in the Himalayas, called Raniket. Although we were to escape the diseases associated with the heat of Allahabad, most of us suffered some sort of climate change sickness due to coming from the hot sticky atmosphere of Allahabad to the cooler, thin air of the mountains. We were warned to group in at least twos along the mountain road, with its over hanging sides, as it was not unusual for men to be attacked by wild animals such as panthers or jackals. Guard duty was always in twos, just with pickaxe handles, the rifles being locked away.

On one occasion, I was woken to take up my stint of guard duty and picked up my pickaxe handle. I saw a group of jackals rummaging around the dustbin area of the cookhouse, but they disappeared almost immediately, as if melting into the darkness, leaving me unsure whether or not they had been there at all. They had and they had left for a reason. I noticed a black head moving slowly behind a grassy mound. It was a panther. Fully awake now, I moved quickly backwards, into the hut and shut the door and raised the alarm. The animal was cornered, on the rocky slope up the ridge behind the huts by several soldiers. I joined them to see what was going on. The panther started to come up the slope towards us, but soon changed his mind when showered with a hail of rocks and stones. It moved away quickly and although I felt sorry for him, I reminded myself to keep my wits about me in the future. I could easily have been that animal's meal. These, of course were not the only creatures. Many a time, soldiers would be walking back to their hut with a plate of food, only to have a hawk swoop down and smash into the plate for a share of the meat, leaving the rest to end up on the ground for the insects or other scavengers. Some of the men would tease the birds by leaving a plate in the open with little meat or a bone on it, tied to a piece of string. The hawk would then swoop down in the usual way and fly off with its prize, only to come to a sudden halt as the string straightened. It would release its catch unless it was lucky enough for the string to break.

Jungle training was to be in the surrounding hills, if you could call the Himalayas hills. It was torture in the heat and thin air. My pack straps were cutting into my shoulders and its weight seemed to increase by the hour. In the oppressive heat of one late afternoon we were marching along a mountain track, bordering a deep ravine with a rock strewn river below. Apart from short ten minute breaks we had been marching for most of the day, expecting a surprise attack by a platoon of our own chaps. Although only training, they would be using live ammunition. We were told not to worry, as they would not be aiming directly at us. We were not impressed. Anyway we started to move downwards, with the trail widening, bringing us right down to the rocky ford of the river. On the other side there was a huge square rock, as big as a house and we made our way across the river towards it. When we were about halfway across, the ambush started. The so called 'enemy' platoon opened up with Bren machine guns and rifles, churning up the water around us and whining around the rocks. Their officer fired at random, at our feet with his thirty eight calibre pistol as we rushed for the cover of the far river bank and large rocks, firing back with our blank cartridges as we ran. Suddenly the distinct noise of a live round was heard, coming from our ranks, narrowly missing the officer. He was not at all pleased and severely criticised our performance under these practice battle conditions, but did not pursue the matter of how a live round was fired. We never knew who it was or whether it was done intentionally. When I told people at home of the training they were amazed and remarked that if it was so tough, why did we do it, why didn't we just fall out. To that I would say you could, if you were prepared to spend a freezing night on a mountain with a rifle that only fired blanks, to protect you from an area that boasted wildlife such as tigers, panthers and all sorts of snakes. To fall out on a march could quite easily mean death. You would only have the natural light of the night to see and guide you on these dangerous mountain tracks, where, if you fell, a leg or arm could easily be broken. Without food you would soon lose your strength. One chap did fall out and spent a night alone on a rock, listening to the noises of the night and the jungle. He was found later in a bad way, having to go to hospital with a mixture of exhaustion and fright. He never returned to the Regiment. The choice was simple - I didn't fall out. I would find that little bit extra to keep going, sing a silent song to myself, think of what to do when I got home, even the hot meal in the cookhouse at the end of the day, any thoughts to take my mind off the task in hand.

Whilst at Raniket, Jackie and I volunteered for a three day trek around Almora, a place my father visited many years earlier. Most thought we were mad to volunteer, as we had, in their opinion done enough marching to last a lifetime. They preferred to stay in camp. About thirty of us followed our officer and an Indian guide into the hillside jungle trail, our packs stuffed with extra food, their weight and the heat making us instantly sweat. We lived rough and slept out on the slopes of the Himalayas, exploring the mountains and their streams, seeing beautiful scenery that would not be possible during a normal man's working life. Overlooking and following a mountain stream we could see a water buffalo lying in the water drinking. Around him were large trout-like fish feeding in the cloudy water, perhaps feeding on his droppings or what he stirred up off the bed of the stream. It was a wonderful sight watching him, marvelling at his long sweeping horns, as he relaxed, seeming in harmony with the fish. The clear skies of the days brought cold nights, making sleeping difficult, so did the mountainside. We would sleep the best way we could, levelling a space on the ground for our sleeping roll and position ourselves in the most comfortable position to keep warm, looking forward to a welcome hot cup of tea in the morning, watching the wind forming snow clouds on the mountain peaks, as we drifted to sleep. We arrived at Almora, but were not allowed into the town itself. We viewed it from the mountainside and I wondered what had changed since my father was there all those years earlier. On the way back, on some of the flatter ground near Raniket, we noticed some small semi-circular, stone buildings called 'Dutch ovens'. I recalled how my father spoke of these and of his unit marching through this area. They didn't have the luxury of lorries for transport in those days and so progress was much slower. These Dutch ovens were built where a camp would be struck, allowing the cooks to prepare meals and form a base for the night.

It was around about this time I was detailed to go to Lucknow, six hours away from Allahabad, with a small cockney chap. We were sent to the Garrison Police Force for railway station and other duties. Outside the designated area were the back streets where the brothels were located and some of the men would frequent these after a few beers. Our job was to police these areas, arresting anyone going out of bounds, improperly dressed, causing trouble or acting in any unsoldierly manner. As we were soldiers ourselves, we found it difficult to do our job properly, we were too easy going, failing to charge soldiers. We didn't want to be in the police and were both too small should any trouble start. The Gurkha officer in charge was not impressed at all and took us into a night club one evening, saying that at ten o'clock we should go in and arrest anyone drunk or causing a disturbance. Well, this was a drinking haunt of the Irish Fusiliers amongst others, all having a good time in the company of local girls. If they weren't drunk then it was only a matter of time before they were and so, we decided we wouldn't hang around. Just before ten we made our way out and had only crossed the road when we heard screams, shouting and glass breaking as the trouble started. Our excuse the next day was that we were chasing some soldiers who were out of bounds, but they had got away somehow. We could see that the officer didn't believe us and he warned us, that if we didn't charge someone soon we would be sent back. The next time on duty, we charged two soldiers being out of bounds. When we were charging them, they calmly stood with their hands behind their backs. It was only after we had finished that they moved forward, showing their rank insignias on their forearms. They were Sergeant Majors and immediately told us we had not charged them in proper Army manner, and so they charged us, taking our names and numbers, reporting us to the Commanding Officer. Fortunately our charges were traded off against theirs and after a severe dressing down by the CO, we were cleared, but returned to our unit and lost our jobs as Garrison Police.

One of the brighter memories of that time was when I met a beautiful Anglo-Indian girl, seeing her relatives off, onto the train. It was eleven o'clock at night and we chatted. She was white with jet black hair and a Welsh accent. She came from a rich family and was taking a tonga (this was a small two seater horse drawn cab) back to her hotel. I felt that at nearly midnight this was unsafe for her and obtained permission from our NCO to let her ride in our Army truck and was pleased that she agreed. I enjoyed being close to this beautiful girl as the bumps in the road shook us together and all too soon we halted outside her hotel. "Don't be too long Streety!" said the NCO as I escorted her inside. A few minutes later a young black skinned man came to fetch her. She introduced him as her brother. I felt shocked as I was not used to mixed families and found it hard to understand how she could be so white and him so dark. We chatted for a couple of minutes, said our goodnights and I returned to the lorry and headed back to our billet.

By this time we were now back at Allahabad where our peace time soldiering was now approaching an end and the monsoon was on its way, preceeded by a dust storm that blasted the barracks leaving a fine film of dust over everything and everyone. The heat was now so intense that virtually all the grass had died, along with the weeds. A dead horse was found near the barracks. It had died from lack of food and vultures hovered around. They would swoop down a short distance from the animal and then walk with their characteristic stoop, shoulders hunched up, reminding me a little of old men, but on reaching the animal they would tear away at its flesh.

One night the monsoon broke and rain poured down. We leapt out of our beds naked, dozens of us cheering and shouting as we stood outside letting the rain wash over us, cooling down our bodies. Most of us had the red itchy prickly heat rash on our bodies from sweating so much in the hot weather and now, the healing rain would perhaps take it away. Within days grass and plants grew on the formerly baking hard ground around the barracks. Leaves and blossom appeared on the trees as the waves of the monsoon rain swept over us - relief at last.

··· Chapter 3 ···

We sent Christmas cards home on October 23rd 1943, so that they would be there for Christmas Day. We were in the Arakan, a coastal area near the Bay of Bengal, Christmas Day in the paddyfields!

The Japanese had been pushing our troops back towards India and this is where their advance had been arrested. We'd left the 20th Royal Fusiliers Regiment at Bopal and joined up with the Fourth Royal West Kents, a Regiment of the Fifth Indian Division, (later part of the Fourteenth Army).

We had travelled by train to Chittagong then across to the rice port of Coxes Bazaar by freighter. We had two barges of ammunition fastened to the sides of our ship as we crossed the Bay of Bengal. I was just pleased that we got across the bay without anyone torpedoing us. We would have gone up like a rocket. The Royal West Kents had arrived from the Middle East, coming overland and down the Great Trunk Road across India to the Arakan. We lined up and waited to board the lorries that were to take us through the miles of paddyfields and scrubland to the Regiment's forward position. I was standing next to Jackie when the CO came along and he put his arm between the two of us, saying that those on my side would go with the Royal West Kents, so for the first time since we had joined up, we were separated.

With us in the 'West Kents' was John Harman, although some of us called him Jack. He carried with him maps of India and had his own sleeping bag. It was said he had travelled extensively before the war, all around the world, being from a wealthy background. Apparently, his father owned Lundy Island. For some time he had been well aware of where we were going, even back on the train in India, when a lot of us had kidded ourselves that we were not going into action, but he knew. He followed our journey on his maps and saw at once where we were heading.

The Arakan was a land of paddyfields with dense jungle covered foothills and was to be our home for the next few months. Small or virtually dried up rivers, called chaungs ran through this countryside, providing water for the paddyfields. Densely covered foothills stood up in the paddyfields like small islands in a sea of rice. Each foothill was its own kingdom, with jungles and wildlife making a home for the animals there. Across the Arakan lay our objective, the Tunnels. These went through a backbone of mountains called Mayu Range, near to the Indo-Burma border. These Tunnels were once built for a future railway, but never completed. We wanted to link up with other British Divisions fighting on the other side. However, it would be late February 1944 before we had advanced far enough to see these Tunnels with the Japs holding the mountain ridges above them. But before then, we would have to push across the Arakan and clear the Japs from their foothill positions.

While we waited to get onto the lorries, there were dozens of native workers throwing basins of water onto the hot dusty built-up road. They collected these from shallow holes dug at the side, each going out into the paddyfields. When we asked why they were doing this, someone said it was to keep the dust from rising in clouds as the lorries passed. Dust could be seen by aircraft or even groups of infiltrating Jap scouts, giving targets for them to attack. Despite their efforts, dust rose everywhere, but we weren't attacked.

It was early December 1943, almost a year since we had set sail from Liverpool. My war had just begun for real. Our jungle training took place, marching through knee high grass without making a noise and making sure that anything that rattled was secured, especially during night marches. This was my first Christmas away from home and I can still clearly remember eating Christmas dinner of roast duck and vegetables, all washed down with a bottle of beer, sitting on a boundary wall to a paddyfield. We were lucky. The men on duty had army rations, bully beef and biscuits.

I still had this feeling of wonder about this whole new world I was experiencing. I didn't think too much about the Japanese. It never occurred to me that I might be killed. That always happened to the other guy. Then we were ordered to take some large tins of bully beef to our company in the foothills. The trouble was that there was a Jap sniper shooting at anything that moved. The Corporal told us to put the tins on a stretcher and cover them with a blanket. He didn't think anyone would shoot a stretcher party. The trouble with the Corporal was that he did everything in a hurry and he did then. I was adjusting my belt when it was suddenly, 'Let's go' and we went. I didn't feel very happy. One of the men slipped over and the tins spilt all over the flooded paddyfield. The Corporal shouted and told us to pick up what we could and as I bent down, my trousers fell down. I didn't let that stop me. I ran with the others to get back. He then told us to take a tin each and we did but my heart was in my mouth the whole time. The sniper didn't shoot. I think he had gone but we weren't to know that.

It was pitch black when we infiltrated behind the Jap lines. A single sound could give us away but we reached the foothills without trouble and dug ourselves in, digging slit trenches and bunkers, but by daylight a Jap sniper had found us. We got over that problem by digging a crawl trench two feet deep. We were out of his sight and safe for the time being, but we had to be vigilant all the time. There was no refund, no second chance.

Don't think I was a hero because I wasn't and don't think I wasn't frightened, because I was. I was scared but you had to keep in control. It was a rotten feeling, creeping through the undergrowth knowing that at any moment a Jap sniper that you couldn't see would take a pot shot at you.

The next day the Battalion's Bren gun carriers rolled up with our supplies and a party of men were picked to go down and unload them. A young chap near me was picked and with the others, he filed away and started to unload, directed by the company Sergeant Major. After five minutes, a barrage of seventy five millimetre Japanese shells blasted both the men and Bren carriers. Several people were killed including the Sergeant Major. A shell landed by him ripping off his face, killing him outright. Another soldier gave a look of shock and horror as a piece of shrapnel smashed into his chest and he dropped dead where he stood. The Bren carriers moved out quickly; none were destroyed, but the unloading party had been knocked about. We were shocked by the sudden barrage of shells. The young chap survived with only minor scratches to his ankle. He was not bothered though and got one of the MOs to dress it and limped off. His leg became infected and he had to be taken back from the front line to hospital and out of the action, for the time being.

The Bren carriers came again the next day and this time I was detailed to the unloading party. I dreaded leaving my position to go. It was a rotten feeling, like an ache in your stomach. A barrage of shells did come over and I dived under the Bren carrier. Fortunately they were wide of the mark and no one was hurt. Our own artillery replied and we heard the shells burn and buzz through the air above us and land with the thuds of explosion, into the Japanese positions. We eventually encircled the Japanese and captured the rice port of Maungdaw on the Naff River in early January 1944. They said it was an important port but it looked like a couple of tin shacks and a jetty to me. We stayed there one night. We didn't get much sleep though. Where we camped, there were some trees with a type of large grapefruit on them. They kept falling onto the ground during the night, with a loud thud, keeping us awake.

There was a huge area of paddyfields but when we were there, the fields were dry and empty. Whether that was because of the fighting there or it was time that rice didn't grow, I didn't know, but there was no cover there. You tried to avoid crossing them if you could, but you often didn't have the choice. You soon learned to look for tell-tale signs, like patches of earth pock marked by bullets. It was a relief to reach the edge of the paddyfield where the scrub and wild rice offered some protection. We preferred to travel along the chaungs when we could. These were lined with wild banana bushes. One day I was crossing a chaung and saw that I was stepping in someone else's footsteps and that someone was a Japanese soldier. They wore these split toe sandals so there was no mistaking those footsteps, what was more he could only have been a couple of minutes in front of me because the indentations in the mud were only just beginning to fill. His footsteps went one way. I went the other.

Beyond the paddyfields were the jungle covered foothills which is where our company had dug in. I was now C Company Runner, attached to Battalion Headquarters. There were five companies A, B, C and D and HQ, BHQ was attached to HQ. The CO was at HQ. So was the signals officer, the adjutant, the medical officer signalmen and runners. Every morning I would hear them calling up the other company, 'Able, Baker, Charlie, Dog, come in please.'

I preferred being a runner; I was happier on my own, making my own decisions. I felt safer. I took messages and laid and repaired lines of communication, sometimes cutting those of the enemy. I carried a little book which the officers had to sign when they received a message. There was no way of avoiding the issue. I would never have got away with it.

On this particular occasion, we had been detailed to roll out a telephone wire, our objective being a sinister dark foothill which loomed high above us. This was at the end of a banana grove that was growing out of the water at the edge of a jungle river bed, that in turn led up to the foothill itself. The wire was to be laid through the undergrowth. The leaves above us grew in such a way that they formed a tunnel over our heads. Our group of men moved ankle deep in water, slowly forward, most of us perhaps expecting the sudden burst of machine gun fire or the crump of Jap grenades. It did not come and the group slowed to a stop. We stood quietly in the water and darkness listening as the forward platoon of 'C' Company moved onto the foothill without a shot fired. A few minutes later we advanced to take up our positions with the rest of them. After the signals had made contact with the new phone wire we had laid, I returned to BHQ with one or two others to stand by for more running duty. The next few days would see me returning once or twice a day with messages to this position. In the days to come Jap snipers would have moved in on positions near the foothill, looking to pick off a runner and perhaps glean some information from messages carried.

I went out early one morning between two and four o'clock with some medical orderlies to collect two bodies from the top of a deserted hill. Apparently the men had walked a few yards down a track, to nowhere in particular and into the path of a sniper's fixed line machine gun on the hill opposite. Somebody had put towels over their faces to prevent the flies getting to them. I could see that one was a sandy haired sergeant. I recognised him as one of the NCO's that helped to sort us into companies when we first arrived on draft to the Royal West Kents several weeks before. The other was an Indian soldier. Both looked as if they were asleep, but had been hit across the chest, by a line of bullets. We eventually got them to the bottom of the hill and they were buried as we stood guard, taking the map reference for the war commission to identify their graves should they want to recover the bodies. Having said that, I didn't give them much chance of doing so in this inhospitable terrain. But they were at least buried which was more than many of the others. As we waited for the men to finish we noticed another group of soldiers out in the early morning mist on the paddyfields. Standing with our rifles ready to fire we recognised their jungle green uniforms as they closed in towards us. This put our minds at rest, for as they got closer we saw that they were one of our own guerilla patrols. They had balaclava hats, faces blacked and most had Thompson machine guns without butts all geared up for close quarter work behind the Jap lines.

We'd been asked to volunteer as guerillas soon after we'd landed in the Arakan but I hadn't volunteered. Well, I didn't like the sound of it. I was glad I hadn't when I saw what they had to do.

After a brief chat and a smoke, which was fortunately hidden by the mist, they went on their way and shortly after, with our job done, so did we.

I was then relieved from my duties and during the couple of weeks that some-one took my place as BHQ Runner, I was detailed to a trench that was the target of a Japanese fixed machine gun. One of the chaps told me what was happening and said that I could dig the trench a little deeper if I liked. When I got in I threw a few shovelfuls of earth out to tidy it up so to speak and settled down. After the first sniping, where the enemy machine gun relentlessly panned the parapet of my trench, the bullets zipping into the soil inches above me as I ducked down, I dug down a lot further. I dug about four feet to try to ensure my safety next time. When the NCO came round he wasn't too happy and ordered me to get an ammunition box or something to stand on because he felt the trench was far too deep, saying that we were here to fight the enemy, not hide from them. I thought to myself, it was alright for him to say that, he wasn't in there when the bullets were flying. The trench in question was itself entered by a crawl trench on the hill and I was warned by some of the other chaps not to look over in the daytime and only take a short look at night. Every now and then, in the darkness, a short burst of bullets would be let off by the sniper in the hope of catching someone off guard. This was a nerve racking time, but I got used to it. I was able to move out via a crawl trench for meals and the like and would often nip into the next trench, which was not the target of the sniper, and was able to spy through a hole in the forward wall of the trench to look for the machine gunner's position.

While I was in my own trench those in the neighbouring trenches would ask me to throw up a cigarette packet to see if they could spot him. I did this by throwing up an empty packet over the front of the trench and each time imme-diately drew a burst of machine gun fire from the Jap. I continually teased the machine gunner into wasting his ammunition, by now and then throwing a shovel full of earth or a stick, over the parapet of the trench, each time receiving a burst of fire in reply. The Jap wasted about five or so of his bullets in each particular burst. I reckoned my taunting over the two week period I was in that trench must have cost him to waste hundreds of rounds of ammunition.

It was boring having to keep low down in the trench all day and I would spend my time banking up the parapet by deepening the trench and carving out holes in the trench walls to form little shelves and alcoves for personal things, such as a tin of jam or bully beef. I had to ration myself to only a spoonful of jam a day, to make it last. The rest of the time I would spend writing letters or reading. Now and then though, my comrades in the next trench would invite me to look through their field glasses to see if I could see the sniper or any wildlife. One day I saw a tiger eating a dead mule over in a distant paddyfield. However, the interest was limited as we had a job to do, but it did break up the monotony and tension of the task in hand.

Many a time the Signals Officer would shout for the 'C' Company runner and my heart would sink. Once, I had just finished my breakfast of baked beans and tinned soya mince sausages, all washed down with a mug of tea. Still tired from lack of sleep after weeks of two hours on and two hours off night guard duty, I was hoping to rest a little after breakfast. Now I was being pushed out into the paddyfields and an uncertain future lay ahead. I grabbed my rifle and bandolier of fifty rounds of 303 ammunition and took the message from the officer. Then I started moving down the track off the hill, to the paddyfields below, passing by bunkers and trenches, with someone saying 'Alright Streety', to give moral support in some small way. I would give a grin and a wink to hide the fear I felt and reply, 'Alright' and then soon I was on my way towards the jungle cover. It was late January 1944 and out there on the paddyfields of the Arakan, little tidal streams and small chaungs moved through the rice fields and I often saw mud fish a few inches long basking on the mud banks, rushing back into the water as I approached. Flocks of green and grey parrots flew over head sometimes landing on the odd dead tree seemingly bringing it back to life with their colourful plumages. They would stand out in the distance above the landscape around the foothills that thrust up their small peaks out of the paddyfields. These small hills some little higher than a house, perhaps one or two hundred yards long, were covered in mini jungles. They were castles that both the British and the Japanese defended to the hilt, each trying to take from one another as we battled for the Arakan.

One Jap patrol blundered onto a foothill held by the battalion, with 'C' Company at full strength and found themselves wiped out. It was dark and they had been challenged by someone in the forward trench. Instead of retreating, the Japs kept coming, led by a huge Japanese NCO wielding a shovel, clearing a path up jungle covered hillside as he went. Most of them were killed outright, but he kept coming in spite of heavy fire, as if nothing would stop him. Then suddenly a grenade exploded on his chest, taking off part of his head and all was quiet again. As 'C' Company runner I arrived on the hill the next day from BHQ with a message. They had buried the Japanese dead, but there was a smell of dried blood and death in the air. I delivered my message to the company commander and stayed for a short while to look at the first Japanese weapons I had seen. One weapon was a type of Bren gun much lighter than ours, with carrying handle going the other way to ours and firing a smaller bullet. Their rifles were longer with a French type bayonet, firing the same small bullets, all strewn about the battlefield, together with oblong leather ammo pouches, grenades, helmets and water bottles and a type of short handled shovel or pointed spade for tunnelling and digging trenches and fox holes. I made a mental note to get hold of one of those shovels as soon as possible as they appeared more useful than ours. I did some weeks later, but only to lose it after a few days.

Shortly after, we infiltrated Japanese lines at night, past enemy held positions. Lucky for us, the paddyfields were covered in mist and we passed through without being seen, to take up positions on some foothills behind the Japs, cutting their supply lines. The Japs soon found us behind them and shelled and sniped our position killing and wounding a number of our men. They were not happy to find us behind them and even more so when our artillery, air strikes and dive bombers turned their positions from green to brown, blasting all the jungle cover away, causing landslides. Their foothill was lost to sight in the clouds of dust and smoke as barrage after barrage of shells smashed into their positions. They would open up with light machine gun fire to let us know they were still around. After one such attack, they retreated one night, using the mist just as we had done, leaving a few die hard soldiers to slow us up. Soon after, our patrols reported no Japs for ten miles and we advanced to our next position.

We had to be alert at all times and took it in turns to sleep, two hours on, two hours off. It was a little easier to move at night but you had to let the others know you were moving. We were all tense. They were a good lot of chaps. We had a lot of cockneys with us and they were always joking. Two of them were great pals. Well, one of them went back to the toilet one night and didn't tell his pal he was going. His friend heard movement behind him and shot him - shot his own pal. When he realised what he'd done, he flipped. He should have been sent back really but there was no way of getting him back. He surrounded his trench with bushes, so no one could get in or out and shot at anything that moved.

I had to tell him to stand to one day. I couldn't get through the bushes and feared he may have started shooting. I wasn't going any closer. I told the NCO why I hadn't gone, 'I'll go myself,' he said and went up the hill.

We all watched and waited to see what happened. There was a lot of wild shooting but the NCO came back after a while and Larry stayed hidden in his trench.

Being a runner I spent a lot of my time in no mans land or behind the enemy lines and had to learn very quickly about jungle warfare as the Japanese were more than experts in this field. Also, I had to keep my wits about me all the time as the thick jungle vegetation of scrub bushes and trees and grasses, sometimes six foot high or more, not only provided good cover for myself, but also for my adversaries. These high weeds could be entered by a small patrol or group of men or snipers that would burrow through a small entrance at the base and once inside, an area could be hollowed out into a small room. The Jap could then wait patiently to strike, even sleeping there under a mosquito net or over a ground sheet, whilst posting their guard in a small hole outside.

It was around this time we heard that the Japs had surrounded the Seventh Indian Division in the pass on the other side of the Mayu Range of mountains. They had broken through some of our forward positions, cut off their lines of communication and swept down the mountain road. The Japs, on their way, overran a hospital, bayonetting wounded soldiers in their beds and chopping off the doctors' hands to prevent them attending to anybody. Our troops were cut off but had formed a box like defence all round, where they fought off Japanese attacks and stayed put until the weaker enemy withdrew, whilst others cleared the area of enemy troops and repaired communications. We now had to withdraw from the hill we held and move to fresh company positions a few hundred yards to the rear.

The new hill seemed more restful, no snipers. We were at platoon strength, with thirty men on this hill and I was still the platoon runner. My bunker overlooked the paddyfields beneath and guarded the track leading down to the platoon HQ and signals bunker. The platoon Sergeant was a regular soldier as were most of the old hands and they had been in action in the Middle East before being drafted to the Arakan. Their experience was vital to the younger soldiers.

Our new position being further away from the Japanese gave us time to prepare. Around the hill was the debris of war, empty ammunition boxes, steel helmets, cardboard, cases and old newspapers, perhaps from the British retreat of a year ago when the advance had failed and the monsoon had forced a stalemate in the flooded paddyfields, for both sides. I decided to set up a dummy machine gun post using two wooden ammo boxes, some bushes and a dummy cardboard barrel thrusting out. Although a Heath Robinson technique, it would be effective to any advancing Japanese soldiers, or at least make them think twice, perhaps giving me a chance to get a shot in first. Finally, I completed it by creating a dummy head of white paper finished with one of the old steel helmets. At night we would cover up surrounding tracks with bushes in order to confuse any Japs or at least hold them for a short time should they advance. The next day the Company Commander inspected our positions and praised us for our work.

Water was at a premium in our new positions as there was no natural supply nearby. However, one of the old hands soon showed us how to get a supply out of the dry paddyfield. He dug a three foot by two foot deep round hole in at the base of a hill. That afternoon the hole was empty, but the next morning it was nearly full of very clear water, gallons of it, that had filtered through during the night. Some of the men dug up turtles while extending and preparing old bunkers for our use and one old hand dumped them in the water hole to keep it clear of insects. Basic but simple.

Many strange things happen during war time and it was round about this time, during action, that we were overlooking yet another foothill surrounded by paddyfields in front of our position. We began to see cattle feeding on the dried out paddyfield and surrounding weeds, or perhaps un-cut rice plants. Young Asian village lads about ten or twelve years old were herding the cattle close by. While we were messing around filling our water bottles they approached us carrying bunches of bananas and jaggery, a form of toffee wrapped in palm leaves and offered to sell us some. We admired the bravery of these village lads. This was the front line, with both sides ready to fire at any time and all they could think of was selling their wares. They made several trips to our lines selling bananas, toffee and on one occasion six foot sheets of bamboo matting which some bought to sleep on during our two hour rest periods after guard duty. The bananas were wild ones with hard seeds in the middle which could jar your teeth if you bit them too hard.

This hill was alive with wildlife. We even had a bear that visited us at night to lick our old bully beef cans and wild jungle fowl were also around. One of these birds really scared the daylights out of me in the darkness, as it strutted through the dark leaves and rubbish up the hill towards my bunker, sounding like a Jap creeping about. It was funny really, my eyes straining in the darkness to see who was there, my finger on the trigger waiting for the target. Then I heard these footsteps turning round a couple of yards or so away and retiring down the hill and the crumpling of leaves. It was only the next day when I saw the jungle fowl strutting up and down the hill in the same manner that I realised what it was that had cost me a night's sleep.

Another night I could hear a rustle of movement in the bushes down in a hollow of trees further down the hill to my right, where another man not on guard, was sleeping in a bunker a little above a hollow. I quietly moved across to the sergeant's bunker asking whether or not I should throw a grenade as there seemed to be a lot of movement which perhaps was the enemy. He agreed, and so I did. Unfortunately, the grenade hit a tree only to bounce off and drop on the roof of the bunker. It rolled off the roof, down the front of the bunker and onto the front of the trench, where it exploded with a loud bang. I had now started something. I heard our sergeant talking on the phone and he then gave orders that the Company Commander wanted to know why a grenade was thrown and ordered us all to stand to and await the impending attack. Most of the men were awake by now, as I moved around to alert them. One group of two men challenged me to halt and give the password. I gave it and the other one said that I was lucky as his friend would have shot me but he himself had recognised my head. I was not wearing my steel helmet, in a rush to obey the order and had not heard their first low key challenge. The tommy gun that would have blasted me away was now pointing safely at the ground and I returned to my position and stood to for an hour. Then the order came for quiet stand down as no attack took place and the next morning I heard and saw the anger of all those that had lost their sleep through my action and they didn't think twice in telling me so.

Later I explored the hollow from where I had heard the noises in the night. Those in the know blamed the bear and set a trap with bedding rope with a slip knot and some bully beef, or rather a number of bedding ropes like clothes lines stretched down the hill and into the hollow all held by three men in the darkness after guard duty. Eventually the bear found the tin and the men pulled on the rope attempting to set the trap, but the ropes broke and the bear escaped, which was a good job really as no-one had given a thought about what they would have done should the bear have been trapped.

We moved on and were now advancing across the Arakan. I was ordered to guide a party of men back from 'C' Company to BHQ. The officer gave me the route I had to follow, which seemed wrong at the time, as it was not the pre-ferred direct route. I could have gone straight through by-passing our old aban-doned 'C' Company position. In this hot climate, with heavy packs and full gear, these men would be very hot and tired having to cover that extra ground and what's more would let me know. I stuck to my orders in spite of the barracking I got from those in my party that knew the route. After a hot and sweaty journey through the scrub and paddyfields I arrived and reported to an officer waiting for them. 'Good, I see you didn't come through the mine field then,' he said.

Again we pushed forward and our next detail was to guard the guns for a few days that were blasting the Japanese positions on the Mayu Range. We moved behind Brigade HQ, a group of us moving into something like the size of a football field with the jungle covered Mayu Range towering in the background. On both our right and left flank was a wall of thick thorn bushes around fifteen feet high and to our front, a road. Flanking the thorn hedge between us and Brigade HQ was a small jungle gully blocked with large lumps of rock at each end. We were here for a day or two's rest apparently, with the somewhat easier task of guarding the guns from parties of Japs rather than front line fighting. Although the guns pounded relentlessly at the Japanese positions we learnt that some seven thousand Japs had been infiltrating along the Arakan among the mountain ranges, threatening to push the Fifth Indian Division back to the Bay of Bengal and promising a second Dunkirk. A group of us setting up camp were ordered to pitch our two man tents in the open. It was felt we were far enough behind the front line and there was no need to dig trenches for defence, for what would only be a night's stay. We wrote some letters and were able to get extra food and beer and generally take things a little easier.

That evening we saw a lot of what we thought were bonfires like camp fires, up in the distant hillsides and there was also a weaving line of flaming torches moving down well away from us. We retired to our tents to sleep fully clothed, with a pack for our pillows and our rifles, ammunition pouches and other weapons at our sides. We even took our boots off, we felt so safe. Bright moonlight and the safety of guards patrolling up and down our tent lines gave us the opportunity to relax and I slipped into a deep sleep, dreaming of the noise of war. I suddenly woke to find the crack pop of Jap rifles and crump of grenades and light machine fire was for real. In a hurry I put my boots on, prepared my rifle and set my bayonet. There was no panic. We were hardened soldiers and instances like this were becoming a fact of life.

The Sergeant Major gave the sentry a thorough dressing down for not alerting the men earlier. We were ordered into the nearby chaung gully near the thorn hedge and a couple of Bren guns were set up at each end with an all round defence of the other weapons to try and secure the area. Each of us was given four grenades and we all crammed into the gully leaving our tents in the open ground. Fortunately, we were quite thankful for the thorn hedge as it appeared that the majority of the battle was taking place the other side at Brigade HQ and no one noticed us, so we simply held our position.

Suddenly a soldier raced up from Brigade HQ shouting for Infantry and was promptly arrested for leaving his post and put under escort within our gully, to be returned to his unit and charged at a later date. We waited for any Japanese attack on our position, but soon the fighting petered out and we stayed in the gully until daybreak. The Japanese had retreated back up into the mountains, and later the artillery spotters located them and started blasting their positions on the mountain side, the fifty five millimetre guns giving them a heavy barrage of one hundred pound shells, turning their green positions to a dirty brown in a matter of minutes, with clouds of dust and landslides to deter them from attacking again. 'No rest for the wicked', one bloke said as we set about packing up our gear and prepared to move to a more secure position to protect the gun batteries. Unfortunately these guns were now only a few yards from us and fired a shell every half hour, throughout the night. We were sleeping in the open and didn't get much sleep at first, but soon got used to it and even managed to sleep through the shelling.

My running duties continued. When I was taking one message, I took a track at the base of the hill and noticed an area of disturbed soil to a bank between two lush green areas, I approached it casually walking, but just as I arrived at the pock marked bank, sprinted through and kept running. A Jap machine gun fired just a second or so too late. Fortunately this machine gun was fixed in position and sited to that small area of disturbed soil and so was not able to follow me. I then went a way up the foothill to deliver my message to Major Shaw, our Company Commander, in his trench. Afterwards, I returned down the forward slope at speed to the chaung and banana grove to safety, carrying on back to BHQ for a meal and rest and perhaps another message. I made many more runs playing chicken with this sniper, each time surviving a near miss.

The scrub lands bordering the paddyfields were covered with weeds waist high, heavy with dew and these would soak my trousers as I pushed my way through. The sun beat down on my steel helmet and beads of sweat trickled down the sides of my face. Already the jungle green shirt I was wearing felt wet with sweat. The Lee Enfield rifle slung over my shoulder seemed to weigh a lot more than its fourteen pounds as I walked towards the foothill where 'C' Company had dug in, facing the Japs on the opposite hill. I felt very much alone and scared as I got nearer to the hills. Suddenly everything went quiet. Birds stopped calling, a lizard with a call that sounded similar to a swear word was silent and all animals seemed to disappear. Then a screaming shell smashed into the paddyfields between the two hills sending up a geezer of smoke and mud.

As luck would have it, 'C' Company had a chaung with four foot high banks, with wild bananas growing in water leading right up to the hill to where they were, then turning off on a new course to vanish into the distant scrub land. After the shell dropped, I took off like a two year old for this cover as more shells crashed down around me. I leapt down the bank, ankle deep in water and headed towards our hill as flying metal from the shells chopped through the banana leaves above my head, showering down bits of trees and vegetation all around me. I waited in the chaung until things had quietened down, before working my way up through a gap I knew, to the lower position where the Company cooks were, at the base of the hill in a high banked, tree covered gully, just off the chaung. Under cover with the cooks, old hands from the Middle East battlefields, they suggested I wait there for a while until the shelling stopped and calmly played cards on a makeshift table of wooden boxes around the cook house area. We all sat there as pieces of metal ripped into the trunks of the trees and branches around us. I watched as a large piece of shrapnel came towards me in what seemed like slow motion, making a strange buzzing noise, as it embedded itself into the tree inches above my head. Later as things calmed down, I raced up to Major Shaw's trench and finally delivered my message.

After handing over the message my habit was to go the quickest way down. Down the forward slope at a run. You run sideways down a hill to keep your footing. I had done this for some days without trouble so off I went, but halfway down a bang was heard and a bullet kicked up dust on the slope about a foot away from my feet. I stumbled with shock but kept going as the crack pop of yet another Jap rifle followed me, but by then I had the protection of the chaung, vowing to change my habits next time I raced back. A day or so later, I was relieved from my running duties and given a rest from that job and found myself with 'C' Company on the hill. This was not to last for long, as the chap who took my place went missing out there on the paddyfields. They decided to make me the runner again and this time it was to be my full time job.

During the end of January and into February 1944, we moved onto a foothill to watch the attack to clear a main large Japanese defensive foothill nicknamed the 'Tortoise', because of its shape, similar to a tortoise shell. Many attempts had been made on this hill to capture it from the Japs. In the past days barrages of fifty five millimetre shells and twenty five pounders had changed the foothill colour from a rich green to a barren brown and at times, the entire area would disappear under clouds of dust.

Vengeance dive bombers had been called in and now a group of these flew up and over, appearing to have passed the foothill as they climbed high in the sky. They then circled and came, screaming straight at the tortoise foothill, releasing their bombs, pounding the enemy positions with their explosions and once more clouds of smoke and dust would hide the horror beneath. As the dust and smoke settled, the Japs would let us know they were still in business and a burst of fire would be heard as if to beckon further attacks. Liberator bombers were also used to break down the Japanese, again relentlessly pounding the enemy.

We at BHQ were asked to watch out for the aircraft recognition panels of cloth that our attacking Company soldiers were to place out, when they had captured the 'Tortoise'. This was to stop further air strikes on our newly held position. After an hour we saw the small figures of our chaps in the distance, laying out panels of cloth in suitable places for our view and a huge cheer went up as this important Jap position had fallen into our hands.

Although the dive bombers helped us with that position, we had a lot of air support throughout the Arakan campaign from two Spitfires who were nicknamed the Maungdaw Twins. These two fighters flew over our positions on a regular basis every day supporting or protecting the ground troops. It was claimed that fourteen Japanese fighters were shot down in a spectacular dog fight high up in the sky over our position. On one occasion we saw many planes fluttering down almost like leaves, but too far away to tell whether they were friend or foe. We were later told they were enemy planes. Another time, earlier in the campaign, I saw two Spitfires flash overhead, heading home, full out, pursued several seconds later by several Jap fighters recognisable by the large red suns on their silver wings and fuselage. No one fired and they were gone in seconds.

The Signal Officer called me and said that I was to take a message to 'C'

Company and pointed to a foothill very close to another in the distant paddyfield. They were almost identical. He said 'C' Company should be on it. I decided not to use the cover of the trees, bush and weeds that grew, in order that I could keep an eye on my destination. I would have to go in a straight line towards the hill or, perhaps, miss it altogether and risk landing in enemy hands. Off I went, straight across the dry paddyfields and hoped that no Jap snipers or patrols would spot me. I set off quickly and arrived safely at the base of the hill and stood and listened at the bottom of a small track, leading up into the jungle scrub of the hillside and heard people talking. I moved up the track thinking our Company had arrived. At the side of the track at the top I bumped into four Indian soldiers in a weapon pit with a large radio set, all dressed in British jungle green uniforms. Straight away I took them for some artillery Operational Unit of our Brigade and asked them in English if the Royal West Kents were on the hill. They looked worried and did not speak and just shook their heads and packed all their equipment away. I felt uneasy and decided not to hang around and re-traced my steps back down the hill. I had just reached the foot of the hill to see our second in command, Major Watts leading a group of 'C' Company men in my direction. 'I see you have got to the hill before us Private Street', he said, grinning at me along with all the others. This embarrassed me, so much that I forgot to tell him about the group of Indians and their radio. Later, we heard that units of the Indian National Army or JIFFS as they were named, were operating against us in this area, fighting with the Japs. It appeared that these Indians were JIFFS. Anyway I passed the message over to Major Watts and headed for BHQ wondering whether it was a near miss for me and considered myself lucky to get away with my life.

Signals Platoon and BHQ Company and the Battalion moved up to a forward position and awaited darkness. When it arrived and the mist fell, we advanced on to the paddyfields passing Japanese positions on the jungle covered foothills. During the first hour out, a lone sniper opened up with a light machine gun, probably hearing us rather than seeing us. His tracer bullets floated high over the column and harmlessly into nowhere. There was no panic and we just kept marching at the same pace moving deeper into enemy territory, leaving the sniper behind, marking his position for others to deal with later. We pushed onto our objective and at first light we dug into paddyfields near a village by the Naff River. By now we had infiltrated twelve miles behind the Japanese lines. Indian troops were to take a village with us in support. The Indian troops attacked the village just before first light, with the aid of artillery support and air strikes. We, ourselves, consolidated our position and waited for further orders. The battle was raging with the crump of mortar bombs, grenades and the crack-pop of the Jap rifles all around. The heavy burst of the replying Bren guns could be distinctly heard. We could see some of the bashas on fire, with others smoking. Then the Signals Officer called me, pointed to the burning village and told me to locate my Company position near the village. I collected the written message and set off across the flat paddyfields towards the palms and other trees closeted around the burning chaos in front of me.

As I reached the village, things looked a bit more disturbing than I had first thought. I began meeting men, women and children, all panic stricken villagers, frightened pale under their tan, fleeing from the nearby battle area. I could hear grenades going off and mortar bombs exploding, together with machine gun and small arms fire. As I had not contacted my Company I headed for the road that went straight into the village itself. On entering, I spotted some Indian soldiers dashing around among the burning huts. One dashed out of the smoke on to the road which passed through the centre of the village. The wild eyed Indian soldier with his fixed bayonet glared at me, but I calmly asked him if he had seen the West Kents around. He looked at me as if I was mad, shook his head as if he didn't understand and dashed back into the smoke which was now billowing around.

I continued along the road out of the other side of the village, onto a built up road passing through open paddyfields leading to a large iron bridge several hundred yards away. I spotted distant movement on the bridge itself and decided to check it out. I thought it might be the new Company position.

I slung my rifle and started out for the bridge along a road which was six foot higher than the paddyfields. Thick bush, rushes and weeds bordered each side. This was the bridge over the Naff River. I could make out matchstick size figures in the distance. I realised that they had seen me and were taking up positions of defence. I had obviously come too far, passed my Company position and had ended up behind enemy lines. I decided not to move away too quickly. I slowly turned and walked off in a normal fashion, eventually making it to a safe distance away, out of range of the enemy lines.

I approached the burning village for a second time and as I looked overhead I heard a roar of an aircraft machine gun and cannon fire. I saw a Jap plane blasting the side of one of our Spitfires. As the Jap aircraft peeled off, the Spitfire trailed black smoke eventually crashing near another village on some distant paddyfield. After further searching, I eventually located my Company, well to the rear of the village and delivered the message as originally requested, and found the reason for the mayhem was due to the Indian troops fighting off the Japanese, who eventually retreated to the large iron bridge, into which I had nearly blundered.

Fire was a continuous hazard in the long, hot, dry periods in this area of the Arakan. The place where we were had a small river flowing through the paddyfields surrounded by an area of bushland and jungle covered foothill positions. A fire started on one occasion, probably caused by mortar fire. This drove a mixed bag of Indian, British and Japanese soldiers off their foothill positions. Our Company cooks on one foothill had just cooked the dinner, as the flames from the bush fire started burning trees and bushes around their position. They were ordered to leave for the nearby river and shelter until the fire had passed, so they dropped the dixies or food containers with the dinner in them, down into deep slit trenches to prevent them from being burnt. On returning after the fire, they served members of their rifle Company a late dinner still hot though, kept warm by the surrounding fire. During this mayhem we all started to cut fire breaks in the area around, sometimes having to dash and take cover in the river as sparks and embers floated over or, wind blown, settled on our packs. Luckily we were wearing steel helmets, but still many were burnt by embers and had to jump into the nearby water to put them out. The war around us stopped for a short while, as friend and foe alike fought nature, rather than each other, to survive. Eventually wind and fire breaks were completed and the fire burnt itself out leaving smoke charred foothills, baring their black peaks. Our positions and those of the enemy were soon refilled and business of war continued.

I returned to BHQ and heard that the fire ridden village was eventually taken by our troops a day or two later. We heard that some more mail had arrived and I eagerly moved forward to collect my letters and a bundle of newspapers. In a quieter moment I started to read the newspapers in my trench, but it was early evening and the Sergeant ordered us to stand to. He said, 'Another day tomorrow Street, to read your papers. Get on with the job in hand'. I put the papers down and leant forward in a position of readiness, rifle and bayonet resting on the parapet of my trench. Another night of lack of sleep was to lie ahead, two hours on guard and two hours off throughout the night, and for all the nights to come. I looked out onto the now darkening paddyfields with mixed feelings and a touch of home sickness.

As the darkness fell the noise of frogs and insects took over. My eyes strained into the darkness as I looked down the track for signs of any danger. This was a way of life for now and many months to come, for all of us here in what we called the forgotten Fourteenth Army, on the Burma front line. As dawn approached, a part of the night time sky lightened. This was a relief to the ones that were forcing themselves to stay awake after days of lack of sleep and the repetitive nature of night guard duty, now almost taking the men to breaking point with exhaustion. As the sun rose, the quiet order to stand down was given. Men still asleep were shaken awake to take up positions of defence all over the hill. This was a quiet morning, since we were on the offensive with fixed positions for a few days. Therefore, we were a little more relaxed as we were not chasing Japs.

We moved next to a small jungle covered foothill sticking up out of the paddyfields, almost as high as a tower block, standing like some castle which, would be protected by its moat in the rainy season. It was now covered in straw coloured rice waiting to be harvested in the later weeks. This foothill was typical of the many stretching away to the distance to meet with the Mayu Range of mountains that seemed to reach up to the sky. Here, we took the opportunity for weapons to be checked and other routine things to be seen to after standing down. These were all the things that were neglected when the enemy were pursuing us.

Here at BHQ the Signal Platoon enjoyed a cowboys' breakfast of baked beans and tinned bacon, with hard biscuits and a cup of tea. As they ate breakfast some signallers were working already, raising the rifle companies and radioing through the orders for the day.

'I say again, Able, Baker, Charlie, Dog. Come in please.' The noise continued to drone into the warm air as others rested, ate and dozed away when their meal was over. The work of the day went on and a call was heard for one chappy or other to attend to some routine duties, but I continued to rest. This was short lived as 'C' Company runner was called over by the Signals Officer to take a message to the Company. I moved down the track to the paddyfields, onto scrubland of the wet knee high weeds and didn't relish another day of wet feet and for perhaps an hour or two, an unknown future. I quickly went to some distant jungle clad foothill where 'C' Company was dug in. But again I was lucky and once again I survived, unscathed, the message safely delivered.

The weather where we were was extreme. An early morning mist and heavy dew would leave the area soaking wet and if I was working at that time the high humidity would drench my clothes and my feet would be wet through. Once the early morning mists lifted, the hot sun would soon dry us out, only for the uniforms to become drenched once more with our sweat a little later. One night we had a tropical storm and us runners were busy putting up rough shelters over our rest area, using branches or whatever was available. Suddenly, John Harman, appeared with a patrol, on some mission or other. He gave me some friendly advice, suggesting I used banana leaves to make the roof more watertight. I only half thanked him for his advice as I struggled with the branches and he went on his way. Those would be the last words he would say to me. He was killed a few weeks later at Kohima.

On another run sometime later, I followed a small high banked stream at the side of the paddyfields, taking my time, watching mud fish five or six inches long run down the muddy banks of the stream, dodging eel holes full of water which moved up and down showing that the eels were at home, waiting for the odd insect or whatever to fall in. The locals would tie a maggot or some such thing to a piece of string and leave it over these holes, waiting for the eel to take the bait. Then they would pull it out with the eel attached. It was like pulling a cork from a bottle. Later, when the war had ended, we would try this method, pitting our skills against the strike of the eel, pulling on the bait and we would give those we caught to the young Burmese children watching.

I entered a chaung leading to our foothill, through a gap in the high bank used by Company cooks to get water for the evening hot meals and tea. Soon I left the ankle deep water and moved on to the semi-dry cover of the weed and scrub on the edge of sun dried, unworked paddyfields and then quickly crossed some open area on the way to BHQ. Near the edge of one paddyfield, I stopped near a paddy bund and could see a distant figure of a soldier, changing course and coming towards me. I hid behind the paddy bund and lay in wait, readying my 303 rifle and focusing it on the soldier. After several moments he came into full view, his English shaped steel helmet giving him away together with his jungle green uniform. Then I recognised him as 'A' Company Runner, himself choosing a Thompson sub-machine gun for his weapon.

We met up and chatted for a few minutes to pass the time and he suggested that we sat down and have a smoke instead of rushing back. After some consideration I agreed, as I normally liked to keep moving. I felt that a moving target was less likely to be hit. Since there were now two of us and good tree cover behind, it seemed a good idea. 'A' Company Runner placed his netted steel helmet between his feet and rested his Thompson machine gun between his legs, holding the pistol grip with one hand and lighting our cigarettes with the other as we sat down. Everything was quiet and peaceful, the call of doves, woodbirds and insects could be heard as we relaxed with our cigarettes. I had done my job, delivering my message and was on my way back to BHQ for a welcome rest. Suddenly, his gun went off, thankfully only a single shot instead of an automatic burst. He had inadvertently squeezed the trigger. This noise, in the quiet jungle, sounded like a bomb to me, as the bullet shot into his helmet and rattled around until it came to a standstill. Fortunately neither of us were injured and the bullet ended up as a flattened lump of metal trapped in the helmet netting. I called him everything as the noise must have alerted everybody in the vicinity. We immediately moved to the cover of the surrounding scrub and got back to HQ.

We continued our push forward towards the Mayu Range, an unforgiving place, which was difficult to map properly, a maze of small peaks and thick jungle, with a network of dry chaungs. Off the road, most tracks were game tracks made by elephants, tigers, panthers and the like. We would hear them at night.

The carnage of war was everywhere to be seen, dead bodies in differing stages of decomposition, all stripped by the animals and insects of the jungle to skeletons. Redundant weapons and equipment lay strewn all over the place. I remember moving back down a chaung with a message and finding a brand new Japanese helmet with canvas cover and net. I looked at it for a few minutes trying to decide whether to keep it or not, but souvenirs of any weight or size were an additional burden, so I left it.

The Japs had dug well into the ridges above the Tunnels and we infiltrated one night by moving through the paddyfields as a Brigade with two other battalions. We moved in the darkness and in single file, by Companies, our mules loaded up with supplies, ammunition and equipment. We marched all night towards the Tunnels area, past foothills and through the dry paddyfields. It was now March 1944.

As dawn broke on the misty paddyfields, a mule let out a loud braying noise and the other mules joined in. At the same time, someone saw a Jap dashing away into the bush and scrub and into the jungle at the edge of the paddyfield we were crossing. We halted and had just started to organise some defensive positions when the first Jap seventy five millimetre shell screamed over our heads, landing on the BHQ area behind us. About thirty shells fell mostly to our rear, as we scraped out shallow trenches in the rock hard ground of the open area of the paddyfield, sweating in the heat of the morning sun. There was a rumble of guns as our own artillery spotter eventually pinpointed the Jap gun and our own shells came over our heads, with a loud burning, whispering sound as they travelled through the air on their way to the Japanese positions. The loud bangs of their explosions somewhere in the hills in front of us quietened down the Japanese artillery and no more shells were fired at us. However, we had suffered some losses, including our Signals Officer's batman and this upset the officer a great deal. The chap who had replaced me as 'C' Company runner was also injured amongst others.

'C' Company prepared to move further forward. We moved to a high ridge-like foothill with BHQ Company. Here there were several old Jap fox holes like caves, all in a line, sinking down inside to about two foot lower than the track. When we struggled in through the small oval entrances, built into the sides of the ridge above the track, we found each fox hole had been enlarged to take three men, able to lie side by side. But the roof very close to our heads made the fox hole very claustrophobic, so I made sure that I would be the last man in and near the opening, when we used them to sleep in at night whilst on guard. The next day we moved to another position and stayed there for a few days and I would take my messages to and from the Company whilst they dug into their new positions, bringing my runs past the remains of the now blown up metal bridge that spanned the River Naff.

As time went by I got used to being a runner and more relaxed, even having a chance to pop in and look at an old Japanese deserted roadside cookhouse, later to be occupied by BHQ, on the side of the road leading to the Tunnels. I used to wander off the road and into the cookhouse and look for anything that might be of value or interest. I only found a pair of old wooden sandals which were of no real use and threw them away. When I turned round I was quite shocked to find I was looking directly into two redundant fox holes, either side of the track which I had just come down. If they had been occupied I would have been shot in the back. I investigated the fox holes further and found that they led out to either side of the road and back into the cookhouse. Therefore, if you chased an enemy through one he could double back behind you.

I was still attached to the Signals Platoon HQ Company, as runner for 'C' Company. Shot at by snipers and near misses from shell fire, out on open paddyfields were all part of the job I'd had, on and off, for three months. This was my third time as runner. The others had been killed or wounded. One was found in a mine field next to the body of a dead Jap. Circling vultures drew the attention of the patrol looking for him. The other was injured in the shell fire on our approach to the Tunnels. We were now moving towards thick jungle and mountain warfare, and so I moved up the chaung with the HQ, taking up positions in the bamboo forest at the side of the chaung and to our right, digging in a few yards from a bend in the dry river bed. To our left was the road leading to the Tunnels about two hundred yards away. These Tunnels were built for some forgotten railway to go beneath the mountains of the Mayu Range. But now they were occupied by the enemy and it was our job to clear them.

Behind the road were the rain forests and the jungles of the Mayu Range. Our rifle companies were digging in on ridges close to the Japanese positions. High above us were well defended Japanese ridges, overlooking the Tunnels. The road to the Tunnels had a dried up chaung to the right hand side, where we were, with a bed of small rocks and gravel, with a six foot high bank up to the road itself, with jungle covered mountains beyond. To the other side of the chaung was a bank of large rocks, perhaps three or four feet high, forming rock pools that stank of the dead fish which had been trapped as the river had dried up. This bank continued into the bamboo jungle.

The reason we had stopped just before the bend was that if we had continued, the Japanese would have seen us. They had control of that part of the chaung and covered it with machine guns from the ridges above the Tunnels. One of our leading patrols had run into some machine fire from the Jap position above. A dead British soldier lay in the chaung and would stay where he had fallen for some time, as a Jap machine gun would be covering his body, perhaps for days, waiting for some of his comrades to come and move him. We waited where we were on our side of the bend. There was no hurry in the dried up river bed and we were well hidden. I would cross the road and then run down with messages as they repaired field phone lines hit by mortar or shell fire. It was essential that any damaged lines were repaired immediately to maintain our lines of communication and we were continuously working to keep things operational.

As we dug in our slit trenches several shells whispered over our heads going towards the Japanese lines. A signaller hidden somewhere in the clump of bamboo trees started to operate his radio set. 'Come in Able, Baker, Charlie, Dog.' I listened to the signaller's voice drifting into the still air in the heat of the chaung. The crack pop sound of the Jap snipers rifle sent a bullet whining down the chaung and a Bren gun answered with a heavy short burst of the recognisable 'Johnny get your gun' sound. The mountains echoed with the thunder of the shells exploding on the Jap positions near us. The signaller from the bamboo clump tried to contact our rifle companies and eventually made contact, as a distant clump of grenades and light automatic fire told me that things were hotting up. Then, someone called for 'C' Company Runner. Now it was my turn to take the risks again up there in the rain forests.

The 'I' (Intelligence) Section Officer was to show me how to get to the new 'C' Company position and we raced across the chaung, with me rushing to keep up with him. We climbed up the bank, across the road and dashed into the jungle onto an old track or game trail, following some lines of communication. We began to move up the mountain side among the trees and bushes, some with thorns that tore at our uniforms as we climbed higher. In parts the ground was soft with a mixture of rotten leaves and stinking mud. The stench was helped along with the sweltering heat of a Turkish bath kind of climate and we were both soaked to the skin with sweat as we climbed. After going up a hundred yards or so, the ground levelled out to a row of privet bushes overlooking the road. The officer said, 'Keep your head down here, we are in full view of the enemy. If you look through the hedge you can see the Tunnels with the Jap positions on top'. We moved quickly past this hedge having a quick look as we passed. I nicknamed this hedge, 'The Privet' and it served as a landmark to me in future runs. The next thing we came across on this game trail was an area of trampled down trees, with football size balls of elephant manure and watery holes in the mud, where their feet had sunk in.

I nicknamed this area 'the Assault Course', as we had to climb over the many tree trunks there, some quite large and eventually got back onto the track again. We continued to climb higher and then to my relief, we started to go downhill and found ourselves back in another part of the chaung, with 'C' Company dug in on a ridge nearby. The Intelligence Officer decided to stay and turned to me and said, 'Well, off you go now Street'. I took off straight away. This was no place to hang about and with a quick look at the Tunnels as I passed the Privet, I soon arrived back at HQ a lot quicker than I went.

I was asked to take a small mixed party of men to 'C' Company on my next trip. Some would stay and about three others from HQ were returning. I was to guide them out and get back as quickly as possible for more duties. For the next few days I would do that trip daily, taking messages, guiding groups of men to and from my Company position, helping to repair the telephone wire damaged by shells. However the first one didn't go to plan. Off we went, with all going well. I made the mistake of telling them how they could see the Tunnels from the privet bushes. I was shocked as they all took a good long look, acting like tourists on a visit to a historic place. I had to be firm and tell them that they could be seen by the Japs and we should get on our way as quickly as possible. We eventually came to the fork in the communication wire and for one moment I could not remember the direction to follow. The men started to barrack me, so I chose one and took the left hand fork. I felt I had made a mistake but was too stubborn to admit it, yet I hoped the wire would lead to a chaung. We climbed up the mountain side and we were all soaking wet with sweat. Some men were swearing and cussing because of the arduous route. We eventually came to a twelve foot dry water fall and I knew by then that this was not the right trail but I dare not tell them, not yet anyway. We climbed the waterfall and continued about fifty yards higher up towards the thicket of high thorn bush which blocked the track. The end of the telephone line lay nearby, it was a dummy line. They all looked at me with shocked faces. We could hear voices behind the thicket itself and they were not speaking English. They were enemy. Some of my men were Eastenders and didn't suffer fools gladly. However, they couldn't raise their voices with the fear of being heard by the enemy, and one whispered a string of verbal abuse, as I had nearly got us ambushed. We quickly cleared off back to the other track before the enemy could hear us, quietly re-tracing our steps back to the fork and onto the right track and onto 'C' Company. I left them there and returned to BHQ still smarting at their opinion of me as their runner and guide.

As the days passed, more and more people used the track past the privet bushes, with more people looking over to the Tunnels and so the enemy shelled the area twice one day. I had to go out with the signallers on some occasions to repair the burnt out or damaged telephone wire on the track. From then on, I kept well clear of the privet bushes, now pot marked with shell craters, neither did I linger anywhere because of the Japanese patrols moving around in the forests nearby. It was a very dangerous area.

We settled down once more and a group of our chaps brought in a Japanese prisoner of war wounded in the leg. We all gathered round to have a look at him. This was the first Jap prisoner of war we had seen captured in the three months we had been in action. He was a small man with a funny beard, that went all round under his chin like a chin strap, but with no hair above his mouth. He looked dirty and dusty as if he had been in action a long time, a bit different to the photos they carry themselves, being neat, tidy and clean shaved in their uniform. The MO and Orderlies had to clear us away and they offered him a cup of tea while the MO checked his damaged leg, but he didn't trust anyone and refused the tea. The 'I' section officer came to help the MO and they decided to move him to a quieter place as many of the soldiers felt hostile towards him. He was then to be sent further back to be looked after and questioned. He would be considered dead by Japanese Army code for allowing himself to be captured.

Our advance through the Arakan had cost us a lot of men. They decided that fresh troops would finish the job. We had had a lot of bad luck really and with the victory of taking the Tunnels in sight, our unit was to be replaced. I was not sorry to leave those hit and miss journeys up and down that game trail. I was pleased to escape the heat and insects. Water was so short that men had taken to sucking roots to help them forget their thirst.

On my last run, I didn't look over the privet bushes that gave the unique view of the Jap held Tunnels, but kept well down and out of sight. I climbed over a four foot high tree trunk, elephant manure and the watery elephant footprints of the assault course, over the slope, still following the telephone wire until I met that dummy wire that joined it. I didn't make the mistake of following the wrong trail this time. I stuck to the right hand trail that led me down to another part of the jungle river where my rifle company were dug in on the mountain side. I delivered my message and went back fast. These Jap infested rain forests were no place to look around as I had done before. However, I did for some reason on my return, take a quick look at the Tunnels through the privet bushes as I passed down to the safety of the chaung and BHQ. This was a Russian roulette kind of life that I had survived so far and to complete that last run gave some relief. But there would be other runs to and from other places in the months to come and I knew this and hoped my luck would hold out.

Fresh troops moved into our rifle company positions towards the end of March 1944 and what was left of our rifle company sections moved out and down the chaung. Our soldiers now had old men's faces, strained and tired under their tan. These were men that had lived a lifetime in a day, seen friends blown apart by shells doing impossible jobs such as fighting and trying to wipe out Japanese bunkers and defences, some of which were not captured. Nevertheless, we had advanced across and captured most of the Arakan up to the Tunnels - not bad for three months work!

··· Chapter 4 ···

We made our way back through the chaung and watched our wounded come down from the rain forests and ridges. We saw friends that we knew on stretchers, like 'Happy' Hamstead from the Black Country. I knew him from training days in Worcester. 'Alright Happy,' we said, as he passed. He smiled weakly and lay belly down on his stretcher, while the MO checked his wounds. Happy Hamstead had his back riddled with pieces of metal from an enemy grenade. I never knew whether he survived. Other men were soon to take the places of those killed or wounded.

Our long column of men moved into a large deserted village, Kaladan, in Company groups, together with a group of mules and muleteers and supplies from Rear Admin. Young men now dusty pale under their tan, had faces that had visibly aged in a matter of months. Some of the sections were down to four men. I remained with BHQ Signals platoon, still retained as Company Runner.

A big mule with a large radio set was unloaded for the BHQ and Company telephones and telephone wires were set up all over the village. Our radio sets were already working, contacting the Companies coming in. The radio operator was already operating, 'I say again Able, Baker, Charlie, Dog. Come in. Able, Baker, Charlie, Dog. Come in.' He continually rattled into the radio set as he tried to contact our rifle companies HQ. We were all busy ourselves, after being allotted our huts. I shared with other Signals Runners and Officers' Batmen. Each of us with a bed space to unroll our bedding rolls, one blanket and a ground sheet, leaving our packs, ammunition pouches, water bottles, on top to mark our place. The cooks served dinner of dehydrated potatoes, mutton, peas or beans and some kind of sweet, all washed down with a mug of tea, which we gratefully took back to our bashas. A few new replacements had arrived, mostly Welsh. They all seemed to be called Morgan, Davies or Jones. We had a good mix of Brummies, Welsh, Cockneys and Kentish men with the odd Irishman, Geordie and Black Country chap. There was nothing to tell that this area of jungle scrub, foothills and paddyfields was on the front line, except for the odd sound of a Jap rifle or the loud bang of a shell burst now and then in the distance. We were back for a rest, more rest between night guards, more time to sleep. We took things easy and received letters and parcels. I received a parcel of cigarettes and chocolate. As I opened it I found that the chocolate bar had melted into a mass of silvery paper and chocolate all mixed up, but I managed to eat a little, spitting out the silver paper as I ate. We got some extra air mail letters and cards to write home. We even had a screen put on the dried paddyfield for a film to be shown by a mobile film crew. Now it seems strange that on that moonlight night, just behind the front line we sat around and watched a film, at first feeling a little uneasy as the Japs had been known to shell these film shows which light up the area in the surrounding darkness. But we soon forgot this and sat down and enjoyed a good film, then away to bed for a good night's sleep.

The next morning someone discovered a large inland lake a few hundred yards away and after breakfast a group of us decided to set off for a swim. We chatted about the good swim we would have, cooling ourselves down, as the sun was very hot at the time, and how we would spend the next few hours, by this lake, swimming, resting and relaxing until lunchtime. We all stripped off and dashed towards the lake like a crowd of eager school boys, waded into the water and kept wading and wading, only to find it was only a foot deep and did not get any deeper. Anyway we made the most of it, splashing about and cooling off.

We were soon feeling more rested and contented and had taken to cleaning our weapons. As we were doing so, one of the lads noticed that on the plaited bamboo ceiling were some very large spiders, as big as small tea plates. We didn't mind sharing our hut with these harmless insects. They seemed content to remain stuck to the ceiling of the basha and never moved, almost like ornaments. The basha itself had no doors or windows, just oblong openings in the wall which served as a kind of window or door. Then a large wasp-like insect flew in through the window opening. It was flying around the ceiling for a few seconds, then lightly settled on one of the big spiders and flew off in one action. Immediately the big spider fell dead at our feet, more or less in the centre of the hut floor. Within seconds we all moved as one, jumping through the window or door openings, whichever was nearer and the basha was cleared of battle hardened troops, in a moment by just one fly. We waited outside for the fly to clear and returned to debate that if this fly could kill a spider in a split second, what could it do to us? We made a mental note to avoid them in the future.

I had nearly forgotten that I was 'C' Company Runner. I had spent most of one day resting in the shade of our basha when the NCO called for me and explained that 'O' (Operations) Group had asked all officers to report to BHQ. I got that sinking feeling of dread for the future as I moved around to alert the officers. After a few minutes it was our turn to hear the bad news. We were to go into action.

We wrote our last letters home, starting,
'Dear Mum
If you don't hear from me in the next few weeks, don't worry;' together with a few silly excuses that fooled no one at home, but we felt it best to cloud the real issue and not to let them worry. We cleaned and fused our extra grenades,

loaded extra Bren gun magazines and extra bandoliers of bullets, rations of food and moved out in company formation. We rode in trucks with some ex-grammar school chaps from I Section, well spoken and rather posh in our mind, but good lads all the same.

We had a sing song as we drove to the airstrip. Then we filed on to the Dakota. It wasn't very comfortable. We had to sit on our packs because there weren't any seats. The crew were American and the navigator kept poking his head out and telling us that if we saw any Japs we were to push all Bren guns through the windows and shoot them. He didn't do much for our confidence, but I couldn't see anything except trees and hills and more trees and hills. We were luckier than the rest of the company. They had mules loaded in the plane with them and they said the animals spent the whole two hours trying to kick the side of the plane out.

We landed at Dimapur. We piled into trucks which headed along the winding, hairpin road up the mountain range to Kohima. We passed bewildered groups of Naga tribesmen, short, sturdy people with a feather tied in their hair and small pigtails at the napes of their necks. Many had red blankets on their shoulders and I can remember thinking that they looked more like Red Indians than Asians. Some carried old shot guns. Others had spears or bows but all of them wore a Gurkha style knife on the hip.

We reached Kohima and had started to dig in when we were told that we weren't needed, so after a few hours, we started the journey back to Dimapur, seventy miles along the mountain roads in the dark. Back at Dimapur we were put on standby and told to make the most of the rest. We didn't have long. The call came at midnight - packs and ammunition pouches on, grabbing rifles and out to the trucks.

We could see and hear shell bursts and mortar bombs exploding and hear the crack-pop of the Japanese rifles. As we got nearer, Asian deserters were running back, shouting and throwing their weapons and ammunition in to our trucks. We were angry when we saw them, but we were told there was a road block further on and they would be stopped and reorganised. We passed trucks packed with men, some of them hanging on to the sides. Others were trotting or walking in the same direction. They all looked frightened. These were the noncombatants, clerks, accountants and storemen.

It was 1st April 1944 and for the past few weeks the Japanese had launched an offensive with one hundred thousand men, crossing the River Chindwin in a big push to try to invade India. The military authorities thought that it was impossible for the enemy to bring an army through the dense jungle and mountains at any sustainable level for combat, let alone in such massive numbers, and so the defences around Imphal, Dimapur and Kohima were apportioned accordingly. The enemy had surrounded the town of Imphal and sent the Japanese

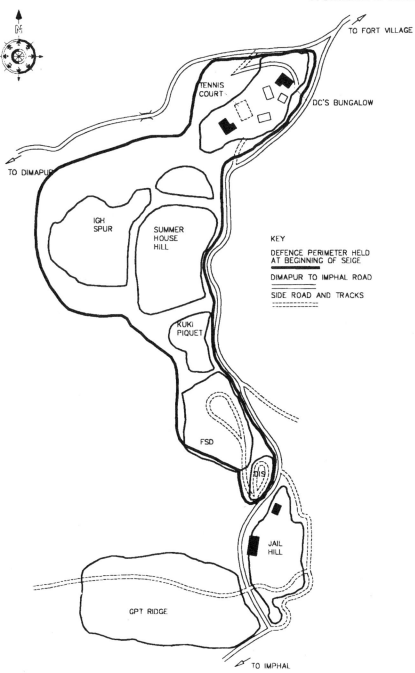

TO FORT VILLAGE

TENNIS
COURT

DC'S BUNGALOW

TO DIMAPUR

IGH
SPUR

SUMMER
HOUSE
HILL

KEY

DEFENCE PERIMETER HELD
AT BEGINNING OF SEIGE

DIMAPUR TO IMPHAL ROAD

SIDE ROAD AND TRACKS

KUKI
PIQUET

FSD

DIS

JAIL
HILL

GPT RIDGE

TO IMPHAL

31st Division north to capture Dimapur and its airstrip. Between Imphal and Dimapur and astride the Japanese lines of communication was the small town of Kohima. The town itself was five thousand feet above sea level and set in a mountain range on the Indo-Burma border. The Japanese would have to take this town in order to pursue their attack on Dimapur.

Kohima was a forward supply depot and a convalescent centre. Kohima itself, had its central point on a road junction between Dimapur and Imphal, a road which turned south and was joined by the Jessami Track. North of the centre, a steep track led to the ridge where a small wooden type fort was positioned. The men dug in around this and the position stretched down to a narrow spur towards the south-east housing the convalescence depot and other small tin roofed wooden huts. Further north among the trees was the Naga village overlooking the township. To the south lay the District Commissioner's bungalow with tennis courts and gardens. Continuing further south was the spur to Summer House Hill and IGH Spur. Beyond this were a series of ridges and hills; Kuki Picquet, FSD ridge (where the field supply depot was built) and DIS (Daily Issue Supplies) Spur which ran down towards the main road. Across the road Jail Hill rose and to the right was another ridge named GPT ridge. The whole area was covered with tall trees. The vegetation was sparse and thin, in contrast with the dense jungles of the Arakan.

The lorries pulled up and the men spilled out, leaving the main equipment on the lorries. We started to dig in straight away. No sooner had the convoy stopped than the shelling started, reducing some of the lorries to burning wrecks. Later, during the siege, some men made daring and dangerous trips to the lorries that were left to get medical supplies and blankets.

BHQ was set up between Summer House Hill and the District Commissioner's bungalow in the old garrison, HQs bunkers. The Indian troops were pulling down bashas and huts to give them a better line of fire.

It was early morning. Ron Clayton, 'D' Company runner and myself started digging in behind a tree. When we'd finished, Ron wasn't very pleased with it. He thought the tree didn't allow us enough field of fire and would give the Japs a target to aim at, so we moved a bit further up the hill and started digging again. We were worn out and lay in our trench to rest. Our redundant trench was in front of us and further on was a long curved trench looking like those of the First World War.

The HQ cookhouse and its defences was to the right; us runners a few yards higher up, in three slit trenches. Behind us, in a big long bunker, was the Signals HQ under the command of the Signals Platoon Officer. A little further back and to our right, towards Summer House Hill, was the BHQ Command Post with the First Aid post nearby. In the pine trees alongside an armoured car lay on its side, its weapon : .issing and huge wheels now motionless in midair. The whole

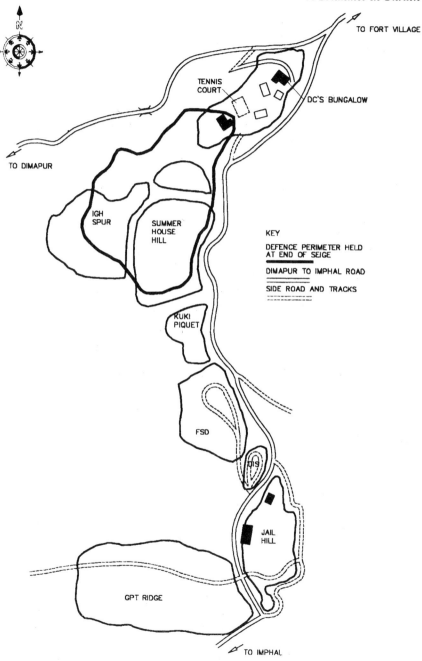

N

TO FORT VILLAGE

TENNIS
COURT

DC'S BUNGALOW

TO DIMAPUR

IGH
SPUR

SUMMER
HOUSE
HILL

KEY

DEFENCE PERIMETER HELD
AT END OF SEIGE

DIMAPUR TO IMPHAL ROAD

SIDE ROAD AND TRACKS

KUKI
PIQUET

FSD

DIS

JAIL
HILL

GPT RIDGE

TO IMPHAL

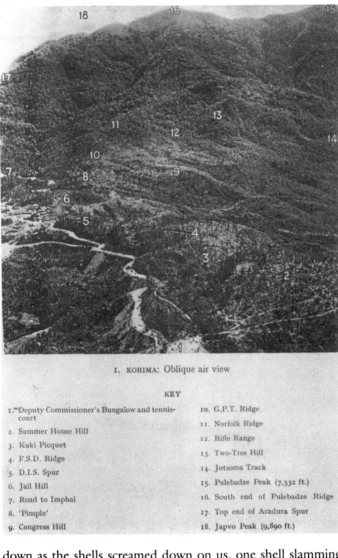

1. KOHIMA: Oblique air view

KEY

1. Deputy Commissioner's Bungalow and tennis-court	10. G.P.T. Ridge
2. Summer House Hill	11. Norfolk Ridge
3. Kuki Picquet	12. Rifle Range
4. F.S.D. Ridge	13. Two-Tree Hill
5. D.I.S. Spur	14. Jotsoma Track
6. Jail Hill	15. Pulebadze Peak (7,532 ft.)
7. Road to Imphal	16. South end of Pulebadze Ridge
8. 'Pimple'	17. Top end of Aradura Spur
9. Congress Hill	18. Japvo Peak (9,890 ft.)

area had become cratered with small shell holes and the litter and rancid smell of past warfare filled the air. A barrage of shells continued into the night and again the next day. I looked out of my trench and a chap that was standing in the doorway of a hut near the water tank suddenly completely disappeared as a shell exploded in front of him. The Jap seventy five millimetre guns must have been very near. We just had time to throw ourselves down as the shells screamed down on us, one shell slamming down in to our former trench, behind the tree lower down the hill. After the barrage we decided to dig deeper and bottle out the bottom on the trench so that we could both lie flat side by side during what seemed to be continuous shell and mortar fire. I think that saved our lives.

Some Indians near us built an open fire when there was a respite in the shelling but the smoke brought more shell fire and the Indians dived back into their trenches. Shortly after that we heard that the Japs had cut off the road behind us. We were trapped, out numbered and under siege. The heavy shelling and mortar fire continued ready for the fanatical charge which the Japs made following each barrage. We could hear them coming. There was this almost inhuman half shout, half scream which they made before they started the charge and continued as they attacked. We were lucky where we were positioned, but the troops in the front trenches were involved in hand to hand combat each time the Japs attacked.

There was a water tank near our trench. At least we wouldn't be short of water and that was a relief when I remember what it had been like at times in the Arakan. We had water for two days, then a shell smashed into the tank. Someone then decided to cover it with camouflage netting. Water was still flowing through the pipe but that only lasted a few days. The Japs captured a position nearby and turned the water off completely. From then on water shortage and thirst was a problem.

The shelling became more' regular, the Japs letting us having it at first light and then again at dusk always followed by frenzied infantry attacks. It was calmer during the day but we had to watch out for snipers or isolated machine gun or mortar fire. We had to be careful all the time.

I looked around in a quieter moment and saw some tethered mules with gaping wounds in their flanks. They didn't seem distressed. They munched steadily at hay but later that day, they had gone. I hoped someone had cut them free and they had run off.

The runs I had to make were different now. For a start they were shorter and they became shorter each day as the Japs steadily pushed us back. I had to move in the dark. It was too dangerous in daylight.

Whilst taking one message at night, I followed a track over the back of our hill through Kuki Piquet down FSD ridge to DIS spur. The sound of someone digging close by alerted me so I slowed down, but it was too late. I was suddenly challenged by a voice, 'Halt'. 'Friend', I quickly replied. The voice in the shadows growled, 'Password'. My mind went blank. The password was 'Chowringee'. It suddenly came back to me and I said it quietly but eagerly. To hesitate over a password could mean death. As it happened, these soldiers had just had a hard time. They were digging a grave for a dead friend and were a little on edge. It was as well I answered quickly, for they were in no mood for anyone like me playing silly jokes.

As the enemy tightened their grip, we were pinned down, unable to wash or shave and we were always thirsty. We used an old fruit tin for urine and threw the contents over the parapet. We used the redundant shell hole as a toilet whenever we could. I don't know how the poor devils managed in the forward trenches.

During the night we got a shower of rain and caught about a pint of water in an old gas cape. We managed to get it into a container, but it was so bitter and the taste of rubber made it so sickly, that we couldn't drink it for fear that we would make ourselves ill. Disappointed, we returned to our trench. Luckily we were sitting down when some Japanese machine gun fire swept our position again. I felt that our trench was taking the brunt of it as the bullets zipped above us and into our parapet. This continued for about five minutes or so. We kept our heads low for the next hour or two just in case. For three nights running, a Japanese mobile gun had been sending shell fire onto our position. We would hear him approach, stop, fire his shells, then start up, move to another position, firing at us again. He was on a road somewhere nearby and we heard him start his engine and drive along to a new position, so that our artillery couldn't get a bearing on him. This became nerve racking as the engine turned over and then stopped. We knew that we would soon hear the screaming sound of the shells. We would hit the bottom of the trench for cover. Each attack lasted for about half an hour.

The battle was still raging, the Japs steadily pushing us back a little further with their barrages and infantry attacks, accepting their massive losses for the small amount of ground gained. My runs grew shorter daily. Japs had overrun positions on ridges all around and 'C' Company had to withdraw back beyond the Field Supply Depot, with 'A' Company just holding their position by the tennis court, just behind the Commissioner's bungalow. I spent most of the day in the trench straining my eyes into the distant roads and mountains, looking for that enemy machine gun that had pinned us down or for a sniper. Some light relief would come though, as a pair of our fighters strafed the Japanese positions in the hills above us with cannon fire and tiny flashes of fire shot up in lines across the hillside.

I soon realised that this was the way of life for all of us here; something we had to live with and these and other dark thoughts would come and go, especially on long night guards. There would be thoughts of food and water, or the lack of it and mainly thoughts of home and the probability that we never see it again. We all had that feeling of not being in charge of our lives, like condemned men. We could not run away, there was nowhere to go and no one was going to take our place or do our job for us. Fate had decided we were going to fight in this battle and all of us had been picked for this period in time. Every man on this hill had been picked by fate and some would die and few of us, if any, would be alive at the end of this siege.

I thought a lot about home, about eggs and chips and going on leave, but most of all I thought about water. I was desperate for something to drink. One day I went across to the cooks and asked for some water. They filled my mug but told me not to ask again. They needed all they had for cooking. I felt mean for asking. The cooks kept us fed, a meal in the morning and one in the evening.

Supplies were being dropped to us by parachute, mainly water and ammunition, but a lot of it drifted across behind the Jap lines. Allied planes swooped through the smoke attacking the Japs, but still they came and our men were being forced further and further back.

Three men appeared, having come down from the command post and stopped by our trench for a chat and smoke. They were in no hurry to go and do the dangerous job they had been detailed to; getting rid of a machine gun post on the road somewhere towards the front line. Their talk was light, of other things, perhaps getting some leave in India, but not their thoughts; we could see they were elsewhere. They appeared not to be really with us. We could see they wanted their cigarettes to last forever. We felt sad as they departed and wished them good luck, feeling thankful that it was not us picked for the job. Sometime later, one of them returned, badly wounded and supported by two other soldiers from a forward trench. When asked about the others, he shook his head and tears filled his eyes. The poor man that survived was badly wounded and had no hope of getting to hospital and he was taken to the sick bay to be patched up as best as the medics could, with the minimal facilities available.

There was some talk of trying to get a patrol through to us, Punjabis or Rajputs, apparently from our own Brigade outside Kohima. They were to get some of the walking wounded out if they could find an unguarded way in. The other wounded lay in a long crawl trench and other trenches all round as sick bay overflowed. The patrol arrived by night and later a party of walking wounded were prepared and taken out the 'back door' to relative safety. Straight after this we were finally cut off and surrounded. There was now no way in and no way out for our troops. Once more the barrage started and continued every morning and evening. The Japs would charge up the hill time and time again, in an attempt to break through.

Tokyo Rose, the Jap propaganda station taunted us by claiming our own army had deserted us and left us to be killed. They tried to get the garrison to surrender their arms in exchange for good treatment. There was silence for a few moments. Then the Bren guns opened up.

We existed with the choking smoke and dust, the bombardment of guns and the attacks from the Jap infantry always preceeded by their maniacal screaming. One morning, a sergeant heard the Japs collecting beneath the cliff and he fetched some grenades and lobbed them one after the other into the enemy beneath him. There wasn't any charge that morning, but when it did come later that day, the Japs seemed even more ferocious than ever.

'A' Company had been forced back to the tennis court but they still held on. They had lost a lot of men. A Scottish private had picked up three automatic weapons from dead colleagues and he emptied each one in turn at the oncoming

Japs. There was no time to reload. They used grenades then to break up the attack and then resorted to hand to hand fighting. We each had four grenades and when they ran short, we gave them two of ours so they could hold out. Those were the conditions. I didn't know how they managed for toilets and the like in 'A' Company but they held their position against incredible odds. The Japs even tried tunnelling under the tennis court to get closer before attacking to prevent losses.

Somehow a Japanese sniper had got on to the hill and was in a tree behind BHQ. Suddenly the top of the parapet and the trenches were swept by automatic fire. We took cover.

Both the CO and his batman were Irish and they were good friends. They used to argue until the CO had to shout at him for being too familiar. They were both characters. Hefferman, the batman, greeted everyone with 'Top o' the morning to you'. When the Jap started firing, he calmly took his rifle, walked in his direction and shot him out of the tree.

There was a case of whisky fastened by a padlock lying on the ground. I passed it when I was taking a message but I didn't touch it. Someone else did. When I went by it the next day, the case had been broken open and the whole lot had gone. That evening, an officer gave us a bottle of rum.

I took a swig and so did Clayton. I began to feel quite merry and I started to sing aloud, 'Onward Christian Soldiers'. Others joined in until the whole hillside seemed to be singing. The officers let us carry on for a while, then gave us the order to be quiet. I don't know what the Japs thought about it, but their attack was not so heavy that night.

The following night the officer gave us some cigars and cigarettes. Three Gurkhas had dug in near us. They had lost the rest of their unit in a counter attack and had been sent back to help defend BHQ. Their faces were pockmarked with cuts and scabs. We gave them the cigars.

They would have preferred the cigarettes but we kept those for ourselves.

Some men had superstitions. There was one NCO who had lost the lucky teddy bear his wife had given him. Finding that teddy bear seemed more important to him than beating the Japs. It seemed that he had almost given up hope of surviving because he had lost it. The following morning he was killed. I was determined I would never get in such a state over a token like that.

My own company had suffered severe losses. I had to take a message to one group but when I reached their hill, there was no one there. It had been a lovely green part of the garden. Now it was just a burnt out dust bowl with a sheet of corrugated iron in the middle. Then the metal lifted and a young officer asked me what I wanted. I gave him the message, which he took in his heavily bandaged hands and drew back into the pit where he and five or six men were sheltering. I asked if there were any snipers about and he pointed at the bullet ridden metal food containers. I didn't hang about.

Apart from ourselves, at Kohima there were hundreds of multi racial group of people moving in and around the township, day and night. Many did not have English steel helmets and some had little or no full British uniforms; most had oriental faces. So it was therefore hard to say if someone unwashed, dressed in this or that were on our side or were indeed the enemy. Many were unable to speak English and of those that could, it was rather hit and miss. Anyway, one night during the darkness, around about three in the morning, three men that I thought were non-combatants appeared. Somehow they had passed through our front line positions and now were standing several yards away from me. I ordered them to halt.

None of them reached for any weapons. I had my rifle levelled at them and they huddled together. They had no means of identification and so I was uncertain what to do. I thought, should I blast them away to find out later I had killed or wounded three, perhaps unarmed, innocent local tribesmen, thus causing all troops to stand to, already deprived of any reasonable sleep, or let them pass. Also, what if the people in the front positions heard someone attacking BHQ. Perhaps there were other hidden enemy troops waiting for these three fall guys to take the fire, thus identifying our positions, so they may attack in force. I was confused and hesitated, but eventually waved them through. They moved on huddled together, with their frightened strained faces looking back, as they continued up to the top of the hill, onto the track and out of sight. The fact of the matter was, as I had not received a password from them, I should have shot them and so in theory, had disobeyed orders. However, nothing was to become of it and fortunately common sense prevailed.

Days before I had learnt that lesson while standing down at dusk and had heard action down by the tennis court in front of us; shouting and fighting. It appeared that the Japs had broken through and were making their way up and through to BHQ. I immediately grabbed one of my grenades and pulled the pin getting ready to throw it at the oncoming enemy. But they did not come and I waited several minutes and realised that they had been held. So there I was, standing with this grenade ready to throw, the pin released and discarded on the ground somewhere. Of course, to throw the grenade would be wasting valuable ammunition and also would draw attention to our position and therefore, we had to look for the lost pin. With me holding the grenade in one hand, Clayton and I searched the bottom of the trench for the lost pin. After about a few nerve-racking minutes, although it seemed an age, Clayton found it, gave it to me and I pushed it back into the grenade. Then I placed the grenade on the parapet in case of further attack and eventually drifted off to sleep. As dawn approached we stood to again and I saw the grenade lying on the edge of the trench with its sprung arm straining to release itself. The split pin had been incorrectly housed with only half of the pin stem being in the correct position, the other half bent out of shape. I immediately went across and withdrew the pin. Whilst holding the grenade handle steady and straightening the pin with my teeth, I eventually made the grenade safe and put it back into my pack.

The Japs continued their barrage on us. It was repetitive and when it was our turn the first mortar bomb would explode about twenty five yards or so in front of us, with a further six bombs slowly working their way up the slope towards our trench. We would count the explosions whilst laying low at the bottom of our trench and after the seventh explosion, jump up with our rifles cocked and bayonets fixed, ready for any attack by any Japs that may have broken through the forward positions. This we had done for the last few weeks. But, fortunately in our case, the immediate front line had always held and the enemy never came. In my mind the siege lasted from the 1st April to 20th April 1944 and everyday at first light and at dusk the Japs would send this barrage and infantry attack to try and break down our defences and morale. We were lucky though, as just forward of our position, about fifty yards away, troops were involved in hand to hand fighting with the on rushing Japanese. We could hear them after each barrage, the screaming and shouting of hundreds of Japs as they psyched themselves up for the forthcoming charge, followed by the shouting and screaming of hand to hand combat. It was horrifying. We never knew whether or not it would be our turn next, as a seventh mortar bomb exploded at the end of our particular barrage. During one such evening, a mortar exploded on the rear of our trench. I lay on the floor at the bottom of the trench and we had at least three more mortar bombs yet to come so would not move until these had all exploded despite the thick smoke that filled our position. The explosion blew dirt, pebbles and earth into the trench and on to our packs. As the smoke cleared we had to stand to ready for any attack that may take place. Fortunately there was none.

Kohima was a depot. There was plenty of food. It was water that was short and it didn't help that Clayton's bottle had been blasted to pieces by mortar fire and we had the one between us. Little things became important in situations like that. Clayton was an officer's, Captain Topham's, batman and he had the officer's kit with him in the trench, including some books about the wild west, just the sort I liked to read and Clayton wouldn't let me touch them, because they belonged to the officer. I really hated him for that. It seems such a little thing now, but there were times when we were standing there, watching, waiting. I would have given anything to have something to read to take my mind off the situation we were in and to forget the dreadful thirst. It wasn't only the lack of water that affected us, but the dryness and the dust and the smoke. The smoke was green and stank of cordite and made us choke.

Apart from lack of ammunition, water was the other main shortage and at various times we were detailed to water parties, collecting water from a nearby supply point in no mans land, tapping a water supply pipe adjacent to the roadway. This was done under the hours of darkness with the men taking turns. On one occasion, I moved with the runners' section of water bottles to join the other shadowy figures of the water party threading their way through the crawl trenches, filled with wounded men. We moved down until we joined the others in the water party, waiting in turn to collect water. Soon it was our turn and one at a time we moved down onto the road. The NCO held the pipe while another man took my bottles, filled them and handed them back to me. A Bren gunner lay flat behind his gun a couple of yards away, its barrel pointing along the empty road towards the enemy should they happen to come along. This was a very tense time, the four of us alone on the road under the noses of the Japs, but it was the only way to replenish our water supply adequately. With our water bottles filled, we quickly climbed up the hillside and, thankfully unharmed, rejoined the returning party, leaving the NCO and Bren gunner there to receive the next group. If anyone deserved a medal at Kohima, those two did.

This detail would continue throughout the night and the pipe would be reconnected so that the supply point was kept secret from any passing Jap patrols, the following day. This operation was done nightly and others would have to take their turn in the days to come to fill their water bottles, but the fear of whether or not to go was easily overcome, the alternative was no water.

The barrages continued, the shelling getting closer. The next barrage started and again we counted the mortars as they came towards our position. Four had dropped when the man in the next trench, a runner called Williams, started to get out of his trench to run, only to be blown straight back in as number five mortar bomb exploded in front of him. The stretcher bearers were called, but couldn't get him out of the trench; it was too narrow, so they had to leave him. It was awful for the poor chap as we could not risk tending to him for fear of being targeted by the enemy, so he was left there until the next day when things had quietened down. Then the medical orderlies came round with a stretcher to take him to the first aid post. When they got there they had to thread a blanket round him, so that he could be lifted out in a sling-like fashion. Although badly injured he was well aware of what was happening and we carried him back to the first aid post. We eventually got him to the sick bay but his injuries were severe and three days later, he died. It was a shame really. He was a good soldier and did his job well. He had served in the Middle East, seeing more action than most. He was a caring kind of chap. It was him that helped a shell shocked runner that came out of a barrage by the Tunnels. The man didn't know where he was and was wandering about. Fortunately Williams grabbed him and helped sort him out. He also helped with the wounded and would often take time out to talk to them as they were carried down.

Towards the end of the siege when the barrage was expected, we would actually look over our trench and watch the first shells and mortar bombs exploding on our forward positions, gradually creeping up towards where we were and beyond. The strain of war began to tell, as during and after each barrage you would hear the groans and moans of those that had been wounded, but we were unable to help. If anyone tried to leave their trench, he may have found himself a victim of mortar fire or a sniper. He then would be wounded, calling for help that couldn't come until darkness fell or things had calmed down.

Although under siege and cut off, the air drops of ammunition, water and various other supplies continued, with Dakota transport planes circling around above, coming in low to the rattle of small arms fire from the Japs. We would then see the small figures in the aircraft push out the cargo and parachutes blossom out and sway in the wind as they fell. Most of the parachutes and cargo landed in the trees and ground held by us. Others floated to the Japanese lines. Some of the water cans tore loose from their chutes and crashed into the ground, bursting the cans wide open, with thirsty men watching anxiously as the water quickly soaked into the dry ground. Some men were detailed to recover the supplies, but were sniped as they did so, as the Japs continued to close their net on us. Our troops retreated to behind the tennis court and Kuki Picquet had now also fallen. Things were looking beyond redemption when we heard that our troops were getting closer. A message came through saying that, should we hold for two more days we would make history.

We held for four.

The sound of our guns, those belonging to the second British Division, were getting nearer and had started to shell the Jap lines. We all hoped that this would weaken their positions and allow reinforcements to get through to us in time. We were told to keep well down, as our own artillery was now massing on the outside of Kohima and would be putting down an extremely heavy barrage, onto the Japanese forward positions just a few yards in front of our own trenches. It was a heavy barrage indeed and it was just as well that we kept right down, for as the shells landed, they shed bits of shrapnel all around us, but we remained unharmed and glad to see the Japs had got a taste of their own medicine. By now our artillery was bombarding the Japanese positions on the hillsides and the enemy forward positions relentlessly, with our reinforcements getting nearer to us every day. But the pressure on us troops was immense and although our losses were nothing like those of the enemy, simple arithmetic showed that it must only be a matter of time before we would be overwhelmed by the sheer number of the Japs. Those two days to make history had now passed and still no reinforcements had arrived, but we fought on. There was no other way.

During the action there had been extreme heroics, probably none more so than that of Lance Corporal John Harman, of 'D' Company. He had been with us since training at Market Rasen. It was said that the Japs had taken over the bakery at Kohima and Harman had approached it single handed under cover of supporting fire, popped a few grenades through the windows and continued on in, shooting and bayonetting the remaining Japs left. Some of the Japs were hiding in the brick ovens, but Harman simply opened the doors and popped a grenade in to get rid of them. Harman came out of the bakery with a wounded Jap under each arm to the cheers of our onlooking troops.

Later, the Japs had taken over a small ridge above 'C' Company's position. Harman decided to counter attack himself. He ordered the Bren gunner to cover him and calmly moved from his trench and walked towards the machine gun nest making no use of the little cover available. He walked from side to side searching for the best position to over-look the enemy. He got a good view, raised his rifle and shot the machine gunner dead. He then walked slowly, still under covering fire from the Bren gunner, towards the enemy, who were wildly shooting back at him. Whilst walking, he raised his rifle again and shot another Jap dead, crouched behind a bush, fixed his bayonet and charged the remaining three, shooting and bayoneting them to death. Cheers again went up from the surrounding soldiers at such a heroic deed, but John simply climbed up the ridge and walked back, despite shouts from his comrades to run. Just before he reached safety a Japanese machine gun caught him below the spine, killing him. He was posthumously awarded the Victoria Cross for his bravery.

It was now the 18th April 1944. Our reinforcements were finally coming. We held on and eventually tanks had now cleared their way through with infantry support to the IGH Spur. The men of the First Battalion of the Royal Berkshire Regiment were first in to relieve us on 20th April 1944.

We gave the advice we could to the newcomers and noted they had new, more modern weapons, rather than the old Lee Enfield rifles with long bayonets. Some had flame throwers. I moved out with Ron Clayton and the other runners to join the remainder of the signals BHQ and HQ platoons and the rest of the Battalion rifle companies, with some of the walking wounded. About seventy of us were still on our feet and able to walk out unaided. I carried my pack, its side ripped open by a piece of mortar bomb that passed through it when the enemy dropped a shell on the edge of our trench, the shrapnel ripping its way through my 1944 diary inside. As we moved down, I noticed that the whole area was virtually barren, the trees and vegetation had been blasted away, just jagged spikes remained of the previous tree cover. Parachutes hung on some of those trees that were left, from previous air drops, their contents long gone. We continued down to a sheltered gully with its cliff like sides finding dead Japs here and there. An upper part of a dead Jap was propped up against the bank in part of the gully, just the chest, shoulders and head, his lower torso and legs were completely missing. The litter of war was everywhere; Jap bodies, helmets and rubbish, everything. We were the lucky ones, thousands were not.

Sherman tanks were now pointing their guns at the Jap positions, protecting the withdrawal and those troops moving up to take over our positions. The trucks waited on the road. Clean shaven drivers and others helped us on. We didn't realise we were heroes then, but the clean shaven drivers and others did. They looked at us in surprise, not expecting heroes to look unshaven, dirty with beards, stinking from the inability to wash and red eyed from loss of sleep. Most of us were lost in our own thoughts and just settled down in the trucks and fell asleep with fatigue straight away, as the trucks trundled down the road. We were woken up for a meal and some tea, then off again, back to the base at Dimapur for a longer rest. We all slept through the next twenty four hours, missing any meals, despite being called and woken up. Soon after, several razor blades were used to cut off our beards, which had grown during the siege and we cleaned ourselves. Twenty four hours later we were called into a large marquee and the CO told us what we had achieved in buying time for others to smash the Japanese advance on India. He told us that he had been awarded the DSO, but it was for all of us, not just himself.

We had two weeks at a rest camp. In a strange way, I missed the bombardment and constant threat for a while. Then we returned to Kohima.

···Chapter 5 ···

While we were still in a rest area, our NCO detailed me and some other men to take over some slit trenches up on a ridge to watch out for enemy aircraft in case of an air raid. The NCO gave me a whistle to blow should I spot any Jap planes. We were allowed to wander around while on duty. We had not seen any enemy aircraft for weeks. Then one day, I spotted a group of aircraft in steady formation over Kohima. Suddenly there was a loud explosion of bombs exploding. I blew my whistle and I raced to my trench. The NCO appeared at my side saying, "Bit late with that whistle, weren't you Street". "I thought they were ours," I replied as we dived into our trench.

The Jap fighters started to strafe the road below and as one flew over our heads I slammed a couple of shots into him aiming at his wings, but he had gone in seconds. Another circled round climbing higher to clear the trees. I sent more shots into his fuselage, but the plane soon disappeared. All was then quiet, the tank guns had stopped, the rifle fire had stopped. A minute or two later I spotted what I thought was another Jap plane flying on the same course. It seemed slower as if searching for a target, coming in from behind a group of trees. I quickly decided to take a really good aim at this one, put my hand up and took the range and fired straight at the cockpit. To my horror, I saw the RAF markings on the fighter which started to waggle his wings to signal that he was friendly. But it was too late, as all the other rifles in the valley opened up. However, the tanks did not fire nor did our automatic weapons as they recognised him immediately. Fortunately he flew off to safety. We didn't see any more planes after that.

It was May 1944 when we moved back towards Kohima and the monsoon was with us once again. We had a new NCO, a hard but fair man. His method of 'on parade, on parade' and 'off parade, off parade', worked well with the men. He was a loyal man to his troops and once, when drinking in a bar with some of them on leave, knocked a chap out for criticising his 'West Kents'. The Japs were now in retreat with many trapped, trying to break out back to their own lines. Others had fled into the hills. We were just behind the front line and could hear the action in the distance. One time, our chaps hit a Jap ammunition dump and we were treated to a spectacular 'firework' display, with explosions and fires burning continuously for three days and nights.

We moved around the back roads above Kohima towards the Jessami track, a route that started by the cemetery with English gravestones and ran through thickly wooded and jungle ridden mountain sides linking Kohima with the Imphal road many miles further on. We passed a burnt out British tank with a shell hole in the back of its turret. It must have been attacked from the rear. Later we moved over an old Jap position and there were about thirty British and Indians on the slopes, just uniforms and bones.

On the top of a ridge was a row of blown out Jap bunkers with their contents looking like something out of a horror film. Dead Jap skulls grinned from under their helmets as their bodies sprawled around on the bottom of the blown out positions. We passed by, happy that those chaps on the slopes had not died in vain. Later on we passed through some of the Worcestershire Regiment positions and I saw some old friends from my Norton Barracks days. One of them was Private Hill and so I stopped and had a rest and natter about old times, during which he dropped mortar bombs down the barrel of his weapon and fired them at the enemy. Without pausing, he would simply adjust the sight and continue firing as we talked. We stayed the night near there and at first light we moved down towards the Jessami track.

We moved in single file down the track. Sometimes we found ourselves at the head of the column with the other members of signals platoon and the CO and other Officers. Mules were the main form of transport, sometimes the only form of transport for carrying food, provisions and equipment on these mountain tracks. For the most part they were only wide enough to let others pass by with very little room to spare. We felt sorry for the mules with their heavy loads. There was a love-hate relationship with them and their Muleteers. Sometimes their loud braying would give away our position, but we needed them. The Muleteers themselves would fuss these animals and scratch around for extra food or titbits to feed them. They got really close to these animals, so much so, I once remember seeing a Muleteer crying, poor chap, because one of his mules had fallen over the edge of track and down the mountain side, dragging the two other mules with it.

After a few days we joined up with one of the SAS type units, fresh faced young lads that had not been in the jungle long, but they had cleared that part of the Jessami track of Japs. One early misty morning at first light, we overran a Japanese camp on the track. The enemy had left in a hurry leaving everything as it was. They couldn't have been gone long. A billy can of water was still boiling on the fire. Rifles were stacked neatly in threes and uniforms were still hanging on bushes. I kicked the tin into the fire and we took the bolts out of the rifles and threw them down the jungle covered hillside. I then went through the pockets of the uniforms for information but most were empty and what we found was of no value.

A dead Jap was on a stretcher and I walked past leaving him alone, kicking a blood stained rag as I went by. My friend behind picked it up and to my disappointment, shook it out to find it was a large Japanese battle flag with a tiger on it, a fine souvenir, nice and light and easy to carry. We searched the camp, but found nothing and started back. That so-called dead Jap had got up and gone. Obviously he was lying doggo and waited for an opportunity to leave. We wouldn't be so foolhardy next time.

Japanese units were still holding the mountain side position at the edge of the road going back to Kohima and, as we moved down, we got a view of the heavy guns firing up at the roadside enemy positions. A few hours later, we had heard Vickers heavy machine guns firing long bursts of fire, again punishing the Jap roadside positions. It was the 6th June 1944, D-Day. We heard that the allies had invaded Europe and although happy, we wished we could get help out here, feeling that we were not getting the praise or back-up we deserved. Helped by air drops of food and ammunition, we moved on down the Imphal Road and, within hours, arrived at Imphal, a town with a British base, airstrip and tented hospital. This small town was situated on the Imphal Plains, an oval, somewhat bowl shaped high plateau, surrounded by mountain ranges of woodland, thigh high grass and jungle. In the monsoon season the plains would flood and look like a huge lake enclosed by the mountains.

We headed for a rest area before pushing forward to clear the Silchar Track, another area the Japs occupied. This track left the Imphal road and went into the mountains, curving back onto the Imphal road towards the plain of Imphal, flat lands of paddyfields with the roadway itself built up high above the surrounding plains. Naga and local tribesmen, mostly women, were on the roadside selling fruit and vegetables in big bamboo plaited baskets, dressed in their traditional red pattern, Indian style blanket, draped over their shoulders, their black plaited pigtails hanging down from either side of their bronze coloured faces. This wild west appearance was completed by the feathers in their hair and trailing earrings. The men carried a shot gun or a spear and most had a tinder box with a flint and would often light our cigarettes for us when the rain had soaked through our clothes, ruining our matches. We reached the rest site and stayed there for a couple of days and were issued with our monsoon capes before we moved up into some high mountains around the Silchar Track. The monsoon season was starting with sudden downpours of rain and spells of sunshine in the day. There seemed to be more rain after dark but I suppose it was the same really, wet and dry spells. As the monsoon continued, the rains lashed at the mountains causing landslides. Lorries slid all over the place and those towing guns were almost impossible to control. Often we would help keep guns connected to the vehicles and on the road by holding onto ropes whilst the driver wrestled with the steering wheel.

In the early hours we moved over the open grassy mountain sides with a lot of dead ground dropping away out of sight. A land of streams and ravines, with very few trees and slippery greasy long grass, eighteen inches high. These were days of never being dry and having permanently wet feet. We would sleep in wet clothes and blankets with water running underneath us as we slept. Small leeches would wave backwards and forwards on the tips of this grass and many found a place inside our army boots by slipping through the lace holes. They would suck our blood, but we didn't feel them as they were crushed in our socks and only discover the tell tale blood stains in our shoes and socks when they were removed. It was the fear of the unknown future that made us take little heed of our discomfort. We accepted it all as a part of the life we were leading; eating, sleeping and most of all, trying to stay alive. We longed to hear those magic words, 'Leave in India'. We would sit on guard each night, on the edge of our trench, half filled with water, ourselves drenched by the monsoon rains and just let our minds drift. It would be perhaps two in the morning and my thoughts would go back to Birmingham. With our time zone being five hours ahead, I would think of what was happening at home; Dad would be getting his last pint of beer to take home from the outdoor before it shut at ten o'clock. Mum would be preparing supper. Then I would perhaps sing a song to myself, or simply daydream of walking home through Birmingham, visualising all the different places, until suddenly, I would hear a noise. My whole body would tense up and I would ready myself, slipping off the safety catch of my rifle and dropping to my knees in our water filled trench, staring into the darkness. I thanked God it was a warm climate as standing in that water for up to two hours at a time on guard duty would have been unbearable otherwise. Slowly I would relax again as all remained quiet and waited to be relieved so I could get some sleep. Sleep would be for two hours as my next stint was at four in the morning, at which time we would have to stand to in case of a dawn attack. Then it would be a quick breakfast of soya sausage links and beans, help load the mules and off again, marching forward towards the Imphal road. I was twenty four years old now, but felt a hundred. All of us young men had seen too much in too short a time. I believe they call it living a life time in a day. I don't know about that, but what we had seen during the last few months was enough for anyone. Home seemed far away, just a dream and then, fatigue would take over, causing confusion. Was this a dream or perhaps was this home. You didn't really know, but you couldn't let these thoughts take over and so, took a grip, forcing them out of your mind. You brought in new ones like a meal at Firpos when the leave that we longed for so much eventually came through. Then suddenly another noise would be heard and the tension returned. I would become a soldier again, no time for thinking.

Our officers in the lead must have had a guide or worked from a map and compass as we climbed up the mountain side. The greasy mud covered the wet grass making the climb harder for us soldiers weighed down with extra rations, ammunition, tents, bedding, cooking equipment and all the other things to keep a busy army unit in action in mountain warfare. The mules in spite of their heavy loads, were sure footed on the grassy slopes and some soldiers hung on to their tails to heave themselves up the steepest parts. Many of us could not bring ourselves to do this, as the poor mules had enough weight to carry, without us adding to their troubles. I don't know what we would have done without these animals, for it was them that furnished us with the supplies that were dropped further back by the American and British planes.

We would rest on that part of the track where we stood and just lay down to sleep in our monsoon capes in the pouring monsoon rain. The mules could not be unloaded and they just stood there. We had a couple of hours sleep or rest; no meals or tea - nothing. I felt sorry for all of us, more so the mules, but we grabbed what rest we could and soon we were called on our way. The column of men and mules left in a long single line along a narrow muddy rain lashed, leech infested track. We were tired and past caring about being hungry and wet as the rainwater poured down our steel helmets and monsoon capes, then onto our uniform, trousers and feet which became wet through. Daylight would bring the hot sunshine to dry us out, but more important, dry our blankets.

When we arrived near the peaks of the mountains, we went along the Silchar Track for a few miles and spread out in suitable defensive positions. We then crossed a deep dry chaung, more a ravine really, with little or no water in it, as there was not much rain now. The early monsoon seemed to have stopped except for the odd shower. We took up our position on a large peak. There were only a few trees around and those were not so high as some we had passed with Jap bunkers dug in under them. We made our BHQ and Company HQ position here. We settled in by the track. Others spread out overlooking the ravine. Thankfully, my 'C' Company were to the rear, a few hundred yards behind BHQ and HQ Company. Other rifle companies were at the front and in flanking positions near us on the dead ground which sloped away. Three feet high grass covered hidden ground around us, but was flattened around the Silchar Track itself. The rain didn't seem so heavy now and I didn't wear my monsoon cape on my runs when taking messages to my Company, just my jungle green tunic, belt, trousers, boots and gaiters, and steel helmet. Most runs were now straight forward. I would cross to a nearby ravine and go along a well worn track sloping downwards at the bottom of the ravine. Then through the wild bushes and small tree growth that grew either side of a little track and continue down this long gentle slope to a dry river bed, that was full of bushes and trees. I would follow this as it wound its way until it became wide open as I climbed out the other side, perhaps thirty feet deep at that point. This was a dangerous place that could hide a lot of enemy troops. The idea of being at the bottom should any

Japs appear in it or on the top was frightening, but, you didn't allow yourself to think of what your fate would be. You did your run and didn't hang around, taking your messages as fast and as carefully as you could. All went well for a few days, until one day, I slowed down as I heard noises in the chaung. I quietly moved forward creeping but lowering myself to a prone position near the edge of the ravine, my rifle at the ready. To my relief I saw three wild pigs, a mother sow and a large boar male pig with a young piglet, all snorting and rooting around in the bushes at the bottom of the ravine. I took aim at the male boar pig but decided against firing, thinking OK I could shoot a pig, but someone may get edgy on the hill and if I miss, the bullet would whine around and could draw fire from anyone, comrades or enemy. Furthermore, odd Jap groups or patrols may be drawn to any outburst of rifle fire. Anyway, the pigs made my mind up for me, getting my scent while I was deliberating on what to do and squealing and grunting they raced off at speed into the bushes, round the bend and out of sight. I slowly moved down into the ravine and returned to BHQ. When I got back I told them about the pigs and they were not pleased. They felt that a nice bit of pork would have been a welcome change to our normal rations.

Before we moved forward, I would be sent to bring the officers of the other companies to BHQ for briefing and to study the mud maps. These were like models of the terrain made from the mud. Then I would have to fetch the NCOs for their briefing.

Another time coming back from a run to my company, I heard a cart or a gun being moved, the rattle of wheel noises in the dead ground near an old Jap position, but the terrain hid what or whoever it was from my sight. I moved up to the side of a peak with the Jap bunkers on top to get a better look and from there I thought I could spot or fire at this hidden gun. As the noise got nearer and nearer from the dead ground, I suddenly knew that I wouldn't reach the bunkers in time. They were too high up. It was clear to me that they would see me first on the open high ground, so I stopped and stayed where I was for a few minutes. I nervously waited and let the Japs continue on their way, both of us hidden from each other's view and then calmly, moved down the track and went back to my company BHQ on the hill. The next day after taking a message to my company I had good news. My leave had come through. They gave a list of places in India that I could visit. This was my first leave in over six months in action and I set off with several other men from my unit to the hill station at Simla. That run was to be my last action on the Silchar Track, for after my leave I was to rejoin my unit on their advance down the Imphal Road.

··· Chapter 6 ···

Simla was over two thousand miles from where we were and to get there I had to travel over land. First I went from the Indo-Burma border and then into India itself, starting with a six hour hike down the mountain sides, with the monsoon already having started. To add to our difficulties we were handed a Bren gun to take back for repair, which was to be left at the Admin. Company, somewhere on the Imphal Plains near the road. A guide led us on our long hike, slipping and sliding and falling down the mountain sides, crossing mountain streams of white water that made it so hard to keep our balance. Although the streams were narrow, we made slow progress to the other side because of the strong currents. As we journeyed on, high above the mountains, we looked down on the Imphal Plains with its clusters of villages and palm trees dotted all over it. The paddyfields were now flooded and it all looked like one big lake, with the mountains stretching into the far distance and out of sight, to India and Burma. We moved down to meet the lorry waiting for us on the built up Imphal road, which would take us first to Admin. Company. Then we were to go by another lorry to Dimapur railway station, past Kohima. We wasted no time getting aboard, but were muddy and needed a change of uniform and socks. When we saw the Quarter Master at Admin. Company we would get these and our money for leave, together with the necessary passes for the trains. We stayed overnight at Admin. Company and then got a lorry onto Dimapur Station the next morning after breakfast. Our group were put under a Scots NCO from a West African Regiment. He was an easy going tall Scot who had seen action in the Arakan with the tall African soldiers of the West African Division.

While we waited for our train, we chatted to him and exchanged stories. The station was packed full of soldiers in jungle green. We stood around in groups chatting, with our bedding rolls and packs on the ground near us when a strange soldier appeared, thick set, in a KD (khaki drill) light off white style of uniform, a pre-war peace time uniform that you see in some of the Indian garrison towns far from the front line. He sported a silver knobbed cane and marched up to us and started telling us how smart his old regiment was. He told us how on parade you had to be smart and march properly and showed us by marching up and down. The Scots NCO grinned and winked at us. He knew what this chap was and nodded at two 'Red Caps'. This strange soldier stood out like a sore thumb in our crowd of jungle green uniforms. The Red Caps marched him away.

Our tins of rations had now arrived and we loaded them on to the train with the tea and sugar and tins of milk for making tea along the way and took our seats. We didn't know it then, but this journey would end at the Brahmaputra River several hours away. From the train, we got onto an old paddle steamer that looked like something out of the old Mississippi western films, as did we all with our bush hats and bedding rolls slung over our shoulders. Some of the officers had 38 calibre pistols on their hips, some tied down in holsters on their thighs, like the old fashioned gun slingers. To me the whole scene was like a picture out of the wild west magazines I used to read as a kid. It was almost unreal. We found a space on the deck and lay out our ground sheets and blankets to rest, using our packs as pillows. We carried no rifles on leave and our small packs had our mess tins, knives, forks and spoons and tin mug for tea. A cooked meal was prepared for us at least once a day on the boat and we still had plenty of tinned food in our ration tins and hot tea for in-between times. We had plenty of cigarettes to smoke and lazy days to get some welcome sleep. There were no guards on this boat and we relaxed. The river itself was very wide, perhaps a mile or so across and was flooded with the monsoon rain. Now and then the paddle steamer blasted off its horn warning, other boats. The echo of that sound gave the feeling of vast space around us, for the river was so big, as too were the fish. We would look over the side and see very large black fish of some kind, that when hearing the steamer coming sank below the surface some yards in front of us. We took it easy while we could and forty eight hours later we reached our destination, another rail head and boarded the train to Calcutta. I caught a cold on this train. It seemed the lazy style of life allowed the dormant germs to force their way out, but I soon recovered. We took our daily mepacrine tablets to keep malaria at bay, our skin now turning yellow with their continual use. When we arrived, we settled into the army rest camp of bashas with their typical Indian wooden string beds with coconut fibre mattresses. An organised cookhouse gave us meals three times a day. The camp had an MO and mod cons, even pay parades and furthermore, our kit was safe in the basha at our rest camp.

After booking in we left to visit the Chowringee. We had waited a long time for this. The Chowringee was a main road of hotels, picture houses, barbers and other places of amusement. Most of us went to Firpos Hotel as it was said to be a place to go. A door with the name 'Firpos' above, guided us up a large staircase into a large long room with rows of tables and chairs in typical English style, with snowy white linen tablecloths. We were ushered to tables, each with a waiter and bearer with white turbans and clean white tunic style coats and red sashes. They handed us the menus and we settled down to a meal of duck with green peas and potatoes, washed down with a few bottles of ice cold beer. After that we went to an air conditioned picture house. As we sat in comfort I noticed a shelf was provided in front of the seats for the cold drinks and these were sent to us as we sat down watching the film. We even went to an old fashioned barber's shop for a haircut, shave and hot face towels. We couldn't believe it, it was like something out of the old cowboy films. However, outside this luxury, beggars would sit around in the street begging for money and we would give them a few annas of change before continuing on our way to join a mass of other soldiers sightseeing, watching the rickshaw wallahs ply for trade and other street traders with all sorts of things to sell. It seemed that the soldiers of a dozen nations were here, Yanks, British, Indians and others, both airforce and army. Some would take the chance to go out of bounds to visit prostitutes in the brothel areas, risking infection. Many got away with it though, not catching anything, but most would stay in the designated area.

It was here that I realised that the world was a small place. I met a chap who lived round the corner from our house in Sparkbrook, Birmingham. He was in some other mob somewhere else along the Burma front line. It seemed quite strange to me that I could meet a person halfway across the world and although he lived so close to me at home, I had never seen him before. Nor did I ever see him again.

From Howra railway station we left to go to New Delhi where for a few coins the local children helped carry our packs and bedding rolls. We boarded our train and got into the carriage distinctly marked in white letters, BORS (British Other Ranks) and after two days arrived at another rest camp to meet our next train. Typically, we had to wait a further two or three days before we boarded this and then off that one and onto yet another, that arrived at New Delhi station two days later.

When we arrived we asked the RTO Officer when the next train left for Simla and found that we would have a day to look round New Delhi before catching an overnight train. New Delhi seemed to be more organised than other areas, obviously because it was near the seat of the British Indian Government, a far cry from the hurly burly of Calcutta several thousand miles away. After a day around the town, we boarded the mountain train to Simla. Once aboard, our bearer stressed that breakfast would be served at four in the morning and we were each woken up with a slice of toast, pot of tea, sugar, milk and hot water all on a neat tray, somewhat different from having breakfast sitting on the floor of the jungle or at the bottom of a trench, rushing to eat in case someone wanted a hand to load a mule or the order came to stand to.

When we reached Simla, we left the train and met the lady in whose bungalow we would stay. We handed over thirty rupees each for our stay there for the following two weeks. Whilst relaxing we discussed and daydreamed of the chances of the monsoon and the wet climate giving rise to landslides, causing the road and rail services to be disrupted, so that we could stay extra weeks while repairs took place - wishful thinking!

A Brummie in Burma

In Simla we got the same warning about staying in pairs as we had at other hill stations, regarding the high roads and overhanging cliffs with the possibility of attack from panthers and other wild animals. All around were pine forests and these stretched towards the wild land around the distant snow clad mountains, miles away in the background. We could look over a small wall and look down a steep slope at the tree tops of the pine forest. The big light grey monkeys were as surprised as we were to see each other and would leap and bound through the tree tops, chattering continuously.

The next morning the lady with the bungalow said we could have as much buttered toast and tea as we liked and we should just call the Indian bearer to get it for us. We had already sampled a bowl of the native form of porridge with milk and sugar. It was horrible. We found a small Indian shop, between the bungalow and the town, that served English food, such as bacon, eggs, bread, tea and coffee. So each day, after a piece of toast and a cup of tea we would make our way to the shop for a full English breakfast. Then we would walk around the town and make our way to the bazaar to do some souvenir shopping. At the bazaar you could buy gifts or clothes to send home and there was even a place to get photos taken of ourselves. I took the opportunity to have a photograph taken and sent it home to my mother and also bought a new bush jacket, trousers and side hat in KD creamy brown. The bush jacket had long sleeves to roll up during the day or to bring down at night to protect my arms from the mosquitos. All this cost only thirty rupees and with free alterations, fitted and ready to collect in two hours.

Simla was a mountain hill station where the Europeans in India sent their families in the very hot months of the Indian summer, before the monsoon broke. The cooler evenings there, the English summer conditions and the clear clean air blowing from the snow covered mountains made it a place for a welcome relaxation, together with its English style churches, bungalows and restaurants. Typical evenings out would be a visit to the picture house followed by a meal. During our stay we were invited to Vice Regal Lodge with its silver throne for the Viceroy and his lady. Other people were in charge when we arrived and passed us over to our guides who were to show us around. These were the native servants and bearers, all of them being thickset Sikhs of military bearing, dressed up in their regal red tunic style uniforms, with gold coats of arms embroidered on the chests and beautiful gold sashes with gold and red turbans.

We were shown around the throne room and admired the large padded armchair style silver thrones. Our uniformed guide trusted us to look around on our own for a while and many of us took the opportunity to try out the silver throne chairs for size. Soon we became bored of looking round the room and our servant guide took us to a large lounge where we had tea and a chat with the relatives and friends of the Viceroy. They introduced us to a dancing troop of

English and Anglo-Indian can-can dancers that were to dance for us. It made us feel like royalty being treated so well by these upper class people.

Unfortunately, our leave passed all too soon and we were back on the train to the front line. On our trip back, we stopped at a rest camp. It was hot and dusty, not like the MacPherson Barracks at Allahabad, with its modern football and hockey pitches and tennis courts.. There, we had the luxury of being shaved in bed in the early morning and our kit cleaned with a fresh change of uniform twice a day, morning and evening, all delivered by the laundry man, or Dhobi, as he was called. It was neatly placed at the end of our beds, boots polished, ready to wear. There was even a barber and a tailor to attend to our needs, and we had hand made shoes for evening wear. There, we had the life of gentlemen and would relax with our charwallah, (tea and cakes), and a fruitwallah on the veranda outside. An indoor plunge/swimming pool was provided and a night time canteen was available. But we did have compulsory bed down after dinner, between two and four everyday at the hottest hours, after which we would have tea. Following that, we would have compulsory sports and then the remaining time was our own, unless we were detailed to battalion guard or picket duties. At night though, in spite of the fans, the air was hot, as the temperature was still very high. You would soak the white sheets with sweat whilst asleep and after getting up in the morning, would leave a wet imprint of yourself on the bedding. This didn't matter though as the Dhobi would change them. Unfortunately however, this place where we were now was distinctly different and nowhere near as comfortable. Simple bashas provided our accommodation, with rough covered toilet and shower blocks.

Soon after we got there we met our old friendly NCO, who had originally come from England to India with us. He was wounded at Kohima and his wound earned him a down grade from the infantry and a safe job on the rest camp staff. He was still our comrade and looked after us well, arranging for a pay parade as we had not been paid for some weeks. Also he told us that there was another train later that week, so we didn't have to rush, thus arranging for us to have an extra day or two at the rest camp, rather than rushing back to the front line. We eventually followed our same route back by train to Calcutta and train again followed by the paddle boat. It all seemed to have gone so fast. We arrived at the jetty to disembark, to get the train back to Dimapur. We had a further night in a rest camp there and then continued our return trip, back through Kohima and Imphal and onto Battalion headquarters.

··· Chapter 7 ···

By now the Japs were well on the run, with many dead or dying; not from death or glory charges, but from disease and starvation as it was their turn to retreat and be trapped. The Silchar track had been cleared of the Japs and we continued our advance down the Imphal road some miles past Imphal. I was still retained as 'C' Company runner. There was no easy way back into the job. The monsoon was still in full swing and I started the next day, doing a run through mud that was so deep it covered my boots. I had to travel from our BHQ roadside mountain defensive positions to the forward position of my company, which was along a trail deeper into the mountains. The roads were thick with liquid mud and the lorries struggled. There was no room for error as there was a sheer drop at the road edge.

We had a rest while another battalion took the lead for a few days and we received some canteen goods, extra canned fruit and a bottle of beer. The cooks prepared some dehydrated potatoes, onions and mutton for the last hot meal of the day, all washed down with a mug of hot tea. Then we took our mepacrine tablets, followed by our rum ration in our mugs, before the guards were set for the night. No sudden attacks were expected, but we still stood to in our trenches. Thousands of Japs were falling back in retreat and were scattered all over the place. We couldn't take any chances. Some of us were allowed to stand down, but other guards remained at their posts and we would later take our turn, in the water logged slit trenches with about six inches of water at the bottom. The two man tents were now pitched on a level piece of ground we had scraped out near the slit trench we dug. These tents were carried on mules during the day as we advanced, but provided shelter when resting in between stints of guard duty at night. As dawn broke we would wash and shave as there was no shortage of water now, the monsoon had made sure of that and we got ready to move on. We had to travel more than three hundred miles over parts of road where battles, past and new, had left bodies in varying states of decay; some fresh, others just bones. I came across what I thought was a dead mule. It was white. The Japs had tethered it to a tree. It had eaten all the surrounding vegetation and even the bark on the tree that it could reach. It died of starvation, poor thing. On closer inspection, I found it wasn't really white, but a mass of maggots eating the rotting flesh. We passed through Tiddim, a hamlet, a cluster of shacks at the edge of the road, with jungle on each side. Then as the road changed with the terrain of valleys and mountains, we approached the Manipur river. At that time I shared our two man tent with a Scot from Edinburgh, a man with a quiet middle class accent. I liked him. We got on fine. I would moan about this and that and he would agree and we didn't fall out or upset each other. That was important.

After the capture of Tiddim, our next target was the Third Stockade further up the Imphal road. This was a Japanese supply base where they kept their food stores, such as sacks of rice, a form of cocoa powder, tins of mixed meat and fish, tinned cherries amongst other things. We had to capture this place to break the supply lines to the Japanese defences high on the mountain sides and other places like the chocolate staircase; a road built up the side of the mountain in loops of hairpin bends, seemingly taking the form of a large staircase. This road and the mud it was covered in, together with its sickly brown colour gave it its nickname. Behind that was a well defended high mountain top called Kennedy Peak. The Japanese could view the road for miles from there. That needed to be captured too. All this was a long way off, near the Chindwin river.

Some miles in front of us, was a twenty mile 'bush' typhus belt, a real concern to the West African Division. It seemed that British troops seemed to recover better from this illness, whereas many of the West Africans died. They were superstitious of these tropical diseases and would give up the fight to live. It was said that it was caught from a rat bug or flea that lived on the tips of the long grass and that these attacked the bare arms unprotected by the rolled up sleeves in the hot climate of the jungle. To combat this, we were given oil to rub onto our arms everyday, to protect us and were ordered to keep our long sleeves down, but we still got some cases of typhus and malaria which reduced our numbers further. However, we moved out in sections, soldiers either side of the road passing bloated dead bodies of Japanese stragglers. Sick and ill, they died where they fell, at the side of the road. The smell of death was with us everyday as we passed these rotting bodies, perhaps friend or foe, you couldn't tell really, just some bones in a uniform, unrecognisable by now.

As we pushed on I met Preston. He lived around the corner at home, in Birmingham and was married with a small child. He had recently joined us and when we stopped to strike camp we would talk of home. I remember that he always sang one particular song, that he sang to his wife - 'Bless you for being an Angel'. It was his favourite and he often sang it whilst putting up the tent or during the singsongs we used to have. He was killed after I left to go into hospital sometime later, apparently shot in error by one of our own chaps, with a sten gun. It was terrible, but these guns were always a problem, often jamming or firing after the slightest jolt. Many a time a despatch rider would ride his motorcycle over a bump in the road to hear the sound of the automatic machine gun fire, only to realise it was his own weapon. Poor Preston however, had been standing in front of a bloke cleaning his gun when it went off for no apparent reason, catching him with a short burst of bullets to the stomach.

We halted for a night near the river banks of the Manipur River and dug in and pitched our tents. There was no bridge over the river here. We heard the roar of the fast flowing river long before we saw it. The flood water was sand coloured and white in places, showing its strength by juggling the tree logs floating down it. A boat appeared from somewhere and some Indian soldiers used to the flooded rivers managed to swim over with a cable to help bring the boat across. I don't know how they managed it as the current was horrendous. Anyway, the rope or cable they took with them was wrapped round a thick tree trunk, on the bank on the other side and a group of soldiers boarded the boat from a pebble beach in a quieter part of the river and began to pull it across. Part way over the boat tipped over and the men fell into the river. It was chaos as the poor men were washed away by the current. Several were missing and patrols were sent to search the banks. Some were found with broken arms where large rocks dragged down by the flooded waters had smashed into them. Those were lucky ones. The others drowned. My friend from Scotland was in that boat and was missing, presumed drowned. His body was never found. It seemed that the water rose up the side of the boat as they pulled it across to the other bank, flooding it and causing it to tip.

I was detailed to go on the second boat and hoped that the people in charge had learned their lesson. We took no chances and took our gaiters off so that if the water went into our trousers it would not be caught by them. We carried all our packs and pouches but they were loose, ready to throw off for us to swim for it should the boat capsize. I had an awful feeling of being expendable but didn't show it. We all got in the boat and settled down. As we waited for the second trip I said a little prayer. The boat slowly moved across the river and as we got nearer the middle the water started to climb higher and higher up the sides of the boat, slowly but steadily. We were worried as it was only inches from the top, but to our relief it slowly dropped again. The rest of the group crossed safely during the next few hours.

There was an open space about thirty or forty feet from the river bank and there I discovered a group of dead Japs. They were long dead, now just bones. I picked up a small ivory rod around three inches long, it looked rather thick like a pen. It was a Japanese family name stamp and I kept it for a souvenir. When everybody was finally across we moved away from the river and up through the rising ground, continuing our advance. Soon, the river became a silver thread of cotton behind us, weaving its way through the mountains. In front of us the road turned into a large horseshoe shape and we moved into a position covered with jungle, bushes and trees and long grass along the mountain side overlooking the road. The valley now lay far below us as the horseshoe road went forward into Japanese held territory. It was four in the afternoon and I was sent on a run with a message to my Company, having to return in the darkness through unknown enemy held territory.

We were told that some local women bearers would help us carry our equipment. We were excited, until they turned up. They were led by an old man in his sixties, with them being 'old hags' in their fifties. Our excitement was short lived, but they were good bearers.

Fortunately, there were breaks in our advance down the Imphal road and whilst dug in on a mountain side, overlooking the road another infantry unit passed through the mountains and around us to take the lead. We were told that we would be resting where we were for a few days. That suited us. During this time we received some mail and made sure we got a little rest and sleep, also taking the opportunity to write letters. The lucky ones got parcels from home and local papers. We also got more to eat here and a bottle of beer from the air drop area, all brought up to us by mules and lorries which worked relentlessly in the pouring monsoon rains. In the evening we had our rum ration and went through the routine of taking our malaria tablets and rubbing ointment into our arms to protect us from typhus. In the daytime we took life easy when we could and on one occasion I walked round and looked at a group of mules tethered to a clump of trees, feeding. They seemed to see me or at least sense me watching. I was perhaps too close to them and they moved almost as one bringing their rear ends slowly in my direction, as if to warn me. I kept my distance as the last thing I needed was one of them to lash out with its back legs and injure me. I realised then, that they too needed time and space as well, so I left them in peace. That evening, Japs started shelling the land near our rest area, reminding us they were still out there somewhere and that they knew where we were. The next day we moved out.

I was still 'C' Company runner and my work was never done. It seemed harder travelling from this rest area in the mid-afternoon, but that was the time I got my orders, to take a message to my forward Company. It was a long hike down the muddy Imphal road with dozens of hairpin bends, with the jungle growing thicker and thicker near the recesses in the curves of the road, fed by the little water courses that trickled down the hillside. I could smell death all the time and once found a fresh corpse of a Japanese soldier that was not there the day before. First, I found this Jap rifle, on the road a few yards away and moved into the jungle to find his discarded pack, then the Jap's body, his head down hanging over the stream, looking as though he was having a drink. I wasn't sure he was dead at first and approached him carefully. But the Japanese diet was rice and taking too much water could make the rice they had eaten swell and kill them. I left after doing my job of throwing the rifle over the sheer drop to the bushy jungle beneath, to prevent others using it, but left the body alone where it was.

Our advance continued down the Imphal road and a muddy mound rose in the road. Stretchers and parts of an ambulance, skulls, helmets, bones and uniforms were all embedded in the mud with our transport still going over it, as we chased the retreating enemy that had not the time to clear the road properly or bury their dead. It was a sickly, awful sight. A British bulldozer was called in to do the job some weeks later, clearing away the stinking mound of bodies, but on that particular day I had to climb over them like walking over a ridge, the mud baked hard in places with bits of body sticking out of it.

Later I would deliver my messages and try to get back to BHQ before it got dark. But it was always dark before I reached this mound of dead and decayed bodies and uniforms. It rose up with its smell of death and although I had done this return journey for days in the dark, my nerves were constantly keyed up, almost to breaking point. Whether it was the place, I don't know, but I always had my rifle unslung and my finger on the trigger, ready to blast any Jap I saw in front of me. It was in fact a very dangerous area altogether and would give the enemy plenty of opportunity to ambush at every deep jungle covered curve and crevice, in the dark corners of mountain bends on that part of the deserted Imphal road. It was indeed a lonely road in the darkness and I would be lucky if I saw one person on my run to my Company and much the same on my return. Then on top of all this almost daily nightmare, which lasted for nearly a week, I had to remember the password when challenged by BHQ guards, hoping they would remember about me being out there in the darkness and not be trigger happy. I would arrive at BHQ and the guards would challenge me, demanding the password. They knew it was me by my shape and voice, but used to pretend they had not heard and challenged me again. I repeated the password, this time louder. 'Speak louder next time,' one of the guards would say. It was all a little game to them, to break up the long monotonous hours of guard duty. They had heard me the first time and I would swear abuse at them as I passed through, with them laughing at my expense. Of course, I couldn't do much about it, as to blunder through, not giving the password could have dire consequences.

We came across a part of the Imphal road that had dropped. It had been caused by a landslide and about one hundred yards or more of the road was missing. I had to climb over the mud and shale slope of the landslide and back onto the road again to take my messages to the forward positions. They later got two bulldozers working on it somehow, one from each end and they soon shaped a new road on the site of the landslide and got the traffic of war on the move again. As the battalion advanced the pouring rain continued to fall. The mud was so deep that it covered our boots and lorries found it difficult to keep on a straight course with a sheer drop to the one side of the road. Ropes were used once again to stop the gun supports, attached to the lorries, going over the edge as they would be lost down the sheer drop, ending up in the jungle beneath. Despite the weather, we could still hear the droning sound of the RAF and American Airforce Dakotas, cargo planes dropping supplies further back at some pre-arranged drop site, to be collected and put on mules to carry up to us in the front line. We would have been at a loss without these Dakotas and appreciated their support, whatever the weather.

One day I left the road, climbing into the mountains following a track which led to a native Chinn village. High on an outcrop of rocky land with a form of dry stone walling and entrance were stone built huts with thatched roofs having rectangular openings for doors and windows. I noticed a fruit tree with quite large fruit, like green skinned oranges. I didn't go into the deserted village. It seemed too risky at the time, but took half a dozen oranges and put them inside my tunic and continued to 'C' Company position further along the track. Here two badly wounded chaps were under a rough shelter with their stretchers off the ground. Both were well wrapped up against the rain and to keep them warm on the mountain side. They would need mules to get them out of there and down to the road using the track. It was a shame and I wondered if it was just too late, whether they were dying from their wounds, just kept free of pain by drugs under the shelter, but this was war and these things went on. I had to take some chaps back to BHQ that were sick or wounded but mobile enough to travel unaided. One of the chaps was called Ingram and I knew him. I gave them some of my oranges to suck, cutting them in half and although they were sour and bitter they ate them. I didn't rush them, but took a slow walk back. It was a dicey track even if you were fit, let alone ill and there were stray Japs about. I was not too happy about that deserted Chinn village, with the orange tree growing near the track. I made them rest for a few minutes while I scouted around the two dangerous bends in the track that could hide an ambush, before I led them forward. I left them and went into the jungle bush and worked my way round the back, to check no one was lying in wait. Fortunately, all was clear and we slowly proceeded forward, going down the open track on the mountain side to BHQ, allowing them rest whenever possible, leaving the village behind us. Later, after the war I would meet Ingram, the chap I escorted down, in Rangoon. He always told others, 'Here's the chap who saved my life when I had typhus on the Imphal road'. I would get quite embarrassed.

Our Company was on the move again. We moved along the road to find an old Jap tank out of action. It had been pushed halfway over the drop at the edge of the road. Further along some flat ground a Jap gun stood idle, its long barrel blown to pieces, sabotaged by the enemy so that when captured, it could not be used against them. The smell of death was still with us and more bodies of dead Japs littered both sides of the road, partly buried in the mud. It was a vile sight, the debris of war was everywhere around. We even found a lorry with a money making, printing machine and thousands of 'Japanese Rupee' notes, with 'The Government of Japan' written on them ready for their troops when they had conquered India. I collected a few of the clean ones to take home as souvenirs.

It was nearly September as we moved forward, climbing higher. There was still heavy rain and showers, although there seemed longer drier spells during the day. My runs to 'C' Company and back went on, the journeys becoming longer. Sometimes I would explore the odd redundant Jap lorry resting in a crevice on a jungle bend along the Imphal road, to see if there was anything of interest, such as information, or perhaps the odd souvenir. It was some road. The town of Imphal was over two hundred miles behind us.

Our next objective was in sight. We were approaching the chocolate staircase. Here the road seemed to take the form of a staircase as its winding hairpin bends climbed up the mountain side, like steps, and its chocolate coloured mud seemed to cover everything right up to the peak. We had some miles to go and halted for a rest. We would soon reach and climb the fifteen miles of road, up the chocolate staircase. The weather continued to get drier with hot sunshine and we could clearly see the endless ranges of mountains disappearing away to India, China and Burma. I was detailed to take another run to my Company in the front line in their mountain positions. On the way, I saw a Jap half track burnt out, no bodies in it, but found a pistol with leather holster attached to a bullet proof steel side panel and took it out for a look. It was a Luger style pistol or automatic, but was too badly burnt to keep as a souvenir, a shame really, so I left it. Passing through the jungle, I began to notice that the water was drying up in these clear mountain streams that came from the jungle covered crevices in the loops and bends of the road. They no longer ran over the road itself and down the mountain side. It looked like the dry weather was coming to stay.

My mind drifted back to times when in previous actions we were trapped in our trenches, with lines of communication cut, the cooks unable to operate during daylight hours, and bully beef, biscuits and water were given and eaten in the small respites of the battles. I could clearly remember, and still can, lying on the bottom of a trench with my comrade taking turns in sucking water off small tree roots and eagerly awaiting for it to be replenished. Now things were better and we made the most of what was available. In war the future was so unpredictable.

We all marched up the chocolate staircase, the other traffic and guns moving up in lorries and on mules, passing some Indian troops moving down. We didn't know where they were going, but there seemed to be a lot of movement of troops at that time. During our march we would look out for water supply points hoping to see or hear some running water. I looked down off the road into the thick cover of trees and the bush in the jungle and luckily saw a wild banana grove and heard water running. The banana groves were a good clue. Their large leaves would stand out to show water, in this case two hundred yards away down the mountain side. I made a mental note of the distance and place as we marched past. We were beginning, at last, to learn the ways of the jungle, recognising a growth of bananas in damp areas around water or a small river and this knowledge would also come in handy for cover during my runs.

High up in this high jungle covered mountain we found a site to rest for the coming evening and night and I was detailed to take a mule with another soldier back down to fill the water tanks. We retraced our steps down the road looking for the banana grove. By then, the sound of running water was quite plain to our ears. We moved carefully down, over rocky rough areas between the bushes and trees and arrived in amongst the banana trees growing out of the limestone ledges. There was our water supply pouring into shallow pools, on a bed of limestone, two or three inches deep. We slowly filled the water tanks and bottles and returned with the mules to our position before darkness set in. The place stank, wild pigs had been foraging and feeding off rotting bananas and vegetation, churning up the mud and mess.

New orders had arrived. We were to go back down to the bottom of the chocolate staircase to the Imphal road, take another route and infiltrate eighty miles behind the Japanese lines. This was a somewhat covert operation, with us leaving the Imphal road at a secret track and moving through the wilds of the mountains and valleys, native villages and the open countryside and hills. We would meet up with groups of natives and soldiers that had operated behind the Jap lines, some of whom had taken jobs for months as tea planters.

We were going to give the Japs a shock, somewhere and sometime in the days ahead as we had brought in a battery of mountain guns on the mules with skilled Indian mountain battery gunners and officers. It may be that the Japs intended to make a stand at the high point on the Imphal road called Kennedy Peak, where they would have a good view of our oncoming troops. If they could, this would give the rest of the Jap forces time to cross the Chindwin River and into Burma. There, they could organise air transport and supplies and give them time to clear their stores and regroup, on the other side of the river. Our job was to cut the Imphal road behind Kennedy Peak and trap the Japs. We marched at night and holed up in the daytime, in places close to the Japanese positions. The weather was still unrelenting as we pushed forward, unloading the mules before first light, digging in to form protection and then trying to get some sleep between stints of guard duty. The noise of the insects and jungle creatures made sleeping difficult, but we got a little. In the late afternoon we would reload mules and be on the march again by the early evening. We passed through many Chinn villages. Their typical houses on stilts were decorated with buffalo horns, quite unusual to us. One particular house that belonged to a Catholic priest, had an English style lawn with a water tap and stood out from the rest. This was a real surprise finding something like that in the middle of the mountains. We continued marching, night after night. Since some of the tracks were so narrow, the mules would scrape their loads against the cliff face causing them to become nervous of the drop on the other side. They would kick and buck as the muleteers struggled to control them. It was difficult for them as the animals were chained together in threes, so if one bucked it was likely all three would become upset, kicking out in an attempt to lose their load. We did lose three mules. The lead mule bucked and panicked, falling over the side, dragging the other two with it, with us all watching in horror as the helpless creatures plunged down into the darkness. A group of men and muleteers were sent to retrieve what they could and returned with some of the loads that could be used, but the poor mules had perished. We pushed on higher and higher up the mountains realising that the only way home now was forward. It was on this march that I tripped over a small rock on the track, catapulting me over and down the side, but fortunately not too far. I was carrying a full pack and equipment and the sudden jolt winded me for a while. I got up and continued, but never seemed to be up to the pace as I had been before.

One night at the head of our long line of men, amongst the high pine forest ridges that flanked the track, our CO and officer stopped to look at the maps more closely with their pencil torch. We had come too far and were in a very dangerous area. The order to halt came and BHQ and HQ Company moved into the wooded ridges to our left, off the mountain track and we prepared to dig in. On the way, we came across a British officer with Indian tribesmen soldiers, making the mountains track wide enough to take jeeps. It was incredible that they were working in this dangerous No Mans Land. Nearby we noticed a dead body of a Jap, only a few days old, sprawled over some bushes. We moved past him and the working party and left them to get on with their work, then we holed up in a pine forest for a few days. Things didn't go to plan, the Japs soon knew we were behind them. They tried to make a stand to delay us and we found that there were many more Japs and transport retreating down the Imphal road than we had realised. This was more than our small group of men could handle. We had been sent just to mine the road, blow up the lorries and then go back to base. So we returned to BHQ, dug in near the track, our rifle company flanking us, with 'C' Company to the rear and awaited further orders.

The runs now were sometimes, twice a day, taking messages to and from my Company. I would go out in the late afternoon and return in darkness, but it was not the same as those past journeys in the darkness, back down the Imphal road. This time I would follow the track, but eighty miles behind Jap lines, in virgin forest. I had to find my own way back in the pitch black darkness, to my Company BHQ hillside position. Up there in the pine forest there were no tracks. This was alright in the daylight as I could recognise trees and shapes or surrounding high points and low points, but in the darkness I only just about made it back after going into a small clearing in the forest to get a better idea of direction. This was more by luck than judgement, as I came into the open area with less trees, which housed our BHQ.

Fortunately, on leave I bought a bone handled Gurkha knife, suitable to cut sapling trees down or use as a weapon. It came in very handy as I took a message the next day. I moved into the forest a few yards and blazed a new trail, not a trail for daylight use, as a Jap patrol could follow it to our camp. So I missed the first few trees and now facing a tree trunk I went behind it and took a slice out, going down about a foot, leaving a light patch. I missed out a further three trees and repeated this action again and several times more, until I reached a small clearing. This again reminded me of the comics I used to read as a child, about the old wild west, the frontier folk cutting trails into the unknown. This together with the 38 calibre pistol, bedding rolls and use of mules seemed to let me appreciate what those American frontier trailblazers thought and did. But now, almost out of the forest and in open land, with a few pines marked up, near my Company position, I delivered the message and when it got dark, re-entered the wood in the same place. Leaving the small clearing I found the first tree and retraced my tracks. It wasn't easy. I found it extremely difficult in the dark having to go back to one of the marked trees to try and get directions. I eventually arrived at the open area of our camp and was passed through by the guard. By my third night I managed to make my way back in the dark quite easily, finding the marker trees a lot more quickly.

We felt our positions must be very near the borders of the Imphal road, since we had telephone poles and telephone wire going near our camp. We were ordered to cut those wires going to the Jap lines and half a dozen of us set off, including some signallers, with a pair of pinchers. They supplied us each with 38 calibre pistols. We left our rifles behind to travel light and set off to a particular telegraph pole in a hollow on the forest floor overlooked by high ridges all round. One of the chaps went up the telegraph pole and found to his surprise, an almost half inch thick telephone wire stretching away to another pole. It was hard going cutting through this with our small electricians pinchers, that would normally be used to cut thin telephone wire or cable, however we finally completed the job. On a ridge high up, we saw a patrol of men, too far away to see if they were ours or the enemy, so took cover behind some trees, pistols at the ready. If they were the enemy, they would be out of range for our pistols, but we would be in range for their rifles. As they got closer we were relieved to see that they were ours, but got a surprise when they told us that we would have been dead ten minutes earlier, if they had been the enemy. They had been watching us for some time while we disabled the telephone wire.

They were a good lot of chaps, our lot. We all mixed in together, the Cockneys, the Welsh and the rest. There was a lad we called James and he spent most of his time with his two friends. Then he was shot in the knee and he died - died from shock. Mind you we hadn't eaten for two days and they said that didn't help. We couldn't believe he'd gone through the Arakan, Kohima and the rest and died of shock!

Some time later I was coming back from taking a message and I found a cross marking James' grave along the Imphal road. I thought I was alone, so I picked some flowers and laid them by the cross and stood there for a little while. Then a voice said, 'Hello Street'. It was the padre. I felt so embarrassed. I don't know where, he came from, we were in the middle of nowhere.

It was nearly October and there was a kind of winter here on these high peaks. We stood to in a foggy cold morning mist in our slit trench, as we heard heavy exploding shells from the Japs in the valley below, hidden from us by the mist. We thought that if they were aiming at us, they were well off target and were thankful that they could not see us. The shelling soon ceased and we heard no more. Meanwhile, our front rifle Companies were in contact with the Japs and we heard the battle going on as our mountain guns opened fire in support. The noise soon quietened and we remained where we were. The next day we made our way down to the road to camp near a river by an old Japanese position and saw a few Jap graves with marker posts in wood, with Jap writing on them. Nearby a small river ran on a gravel bed and I decided to wash myself. I found a lump on my left side and went to see the MO. I had developed a hernia, prob- ably when I fell off the track, half asleep with exhaustion, during the march further back in the mountains behind the Imphal road. But this problem was to be dealt with later and we marched on for a few hours to stay in a teak forest by the former Jap base camp. My hernia would need surgery but I couldn't leave for hospital, as the airstrip was still to be captured. We rested in our tents at this old supply camp, camping near the sandy track. The large high trunks of the teak trees had no low branches and I remember thinking that this was just as well, as I noticed a python hanging from one of the higher boughs.

We pitched our tent near this tree as we felt that the snake was well out of the way up there. However, in the fine sandy tracks all around were a mass of snake trails from snakes of all sizes. Most of the snakes were small, perhaps a foot long and we hoped they were not poisonous. To be bitten out here would probably be fatal. Seeing this reminded me of a four foot long grass snake with a bright red head, that surprised me up in the mountains. The snake came out of the bushes and went under a tent wall and I happened to see it as I cleared some ground nearby. I dashed round the other side and cut its head off, with one swing of the spade, only to find out later it was simply harmless and at that I felt quite guilty for killing the poor reptile.

While we were at this former Japanese camp I took the opportunity to look round. The NCO reminded me to watch out as there could be some Jap stragglers hanging about in the jungle around and so I remained cautious. I saw two natives loading some of the stores that had been left behind by the enemy onto their bullock cart. The cart was full and one of them was on the cart, the other nearby. They looked very worried but I thought they looked Burmese. Their hands were under their gowns and they could have been secreting weapons, I didn't know. My rifle was slung over my shoulder. I had the choice of either playing it cool and taking no notice or unslinging my rifle and risk getting killed before capturing them. I decided to play it cool and let them go on their way. The other native quickly jumped on to the bullock cart and they whipped the two bullocks and raced away. Good luck to them.

As I looked round I saw broken Jap rifles and looking more closely I saw a half buried piece of paper and so I gently dug it out. Someone had obviously buried it in a hurry before they left and as it happened, it turned out to be two military Japanese maps, beautifully coloured, showing the sea and coastline of either Burma or China, all neatly written in Japanese. They were two feet wide, so I carefully folded them up and put them into my pocket and later handed them in to 'I' Section. As I continued, I found a rifle not damaged except for the bolt missing and its barrel packed with mud. Nearby, leather pouches of Jap rifle bullets were tipped out on the ground and so I retrieved a bolt from another damaged rifle and loaded this particular weapon, with a few of the Jap bullets. Clearing the rifle barrel with a bullet, I quickly moved into the forest and fired a few shots at various targets, before returning to camp, realising that the noise of an enemy rifle may attract others.

··· Chapter 8 ···

It was during October 1944 when the nearby air strip was captured that I was flown to Imphal for treatment. I waited for pay parade and went sick the next day, reporting my hernia. The hospital at Imphal was a large tented hospital, but the other wounded men and urgent cases took priority, so it was decided I would be treated elsewhere. After a week I was flown to a hospital in Chittagong, a coastal town near the Bay of Bengal. They did not do the operation because of the lack of facilities. I spent a further two weeks of relaxation and rest on the sandy beaches nearby, swimming in the warm sea. Eventually I was taken by hospital ship to Madras and had my operation just before Christmas 1944.

Whilst recovering, I contracted dysentery and malaria. It seemed ironic really, that I would nearly die of disease after surviving battles of the Arakan, Kohima and the Imphal road. But this was not unusual in South East Asia where disease accounted for many of our losses.

In January 1945 Lady Mountbatten visited the hospital. I had not long had my operation and was lying flat on my back. I was hoping she would pass me by, but the nurse or someone must have said I was a member of the Fourth Royal West Kents, back from the actions of Kohima and the Imphal road. Well, she made a beeline for me. I wanted to sink through the floor rather than meet her, but she smiled and chatted with me, asking if I had seen her husband, then in charge of the South East Asia Command. I said that I had, but reminded her that every time we did, we seemed to be back in action again. She went on to tell me how Lord Mountbatten thought the world of us soldiers out here and really appreciated all the good work we had done. Wishing me well, she passed on to chat to the others. Several days later though, the ward sister told me that someone had been asking about me and when I asked who it was she said she was not allowed to say, but that they were very important. Anyway, she brought me a form to fill in and I was given special leave for a month in England.

However, I was to wait several weeks and was discharged from hospital around April 1945 and sent to the convalescence depot in the Wellington Hills near Madras. After a couple of weeks of taking it easy and doing light duties, such as laying tables, the NCO came to me to tell me my leave had come through. He added that when I was fit and ready to travel, I could take one month's home leave and be downgraded for an easier job when I returned. When the time came, it took me seventeen days to get back to England, but fortunately for me, my leave did not start until I arrived back, so I enjoyed VE Day in England before making the seventeen day trip back to Bombay. Arriving home had been traumatic in itself. At a family gathering I began to feel strange. Everything seemed unreal. My parents looked old and grey since I saw them last. Eventually things became so confused that I burst into tears. After a few minutes I was alright, but it appeared that the pressures of the last few months had finally surfaced. My mother got in touch with a local MP complaining that I was not fit enough to return to the front line. They even got an army MO to check me over, but he said it was too late for him to do anything about it and that I should speak to someone when I got back, to arrange for a downgrade and obtain an easier job in India, rather than the Burma front line. I wasn't bothered but my mother was.

I remember on one occasion on home leave, I was on a bus with one of my aunts, laughing and joking, when a woman came across saying I should not be acting up like I was, as there was a war on and I should be out there fighting. Well, before I knew what was going on, my aunt gave her such a dressing down, telling her where I had been and what I had been through. I nearly ended up having to separate the pair of them.

The leave ended all too quickly and we went by train to Glasgow to catch the troopship, 'The Queen of Bermuda' to Bombay. It was horrible when the train started to leave the station, just after husbands had left their wives and perhaps children, in tearful farewells. Some of the poor blokes couldn't bring themselves to speak for half an hour or so, others were virtually in tears. Us single men left them to thaw out and would joke and mess about, talk about leave and play cards. The others joined in when they were ready. A mix up took place in Bombay and instead of having a soft job I was now being sent back to Calcutta and on to Rangoon, to the front line with my Company. It was my own fault really. All of us soldiers were lined up waiting to go back to our units, when the sergeant asked me which Regiment I was from. I felt I couldn't say that I ought to be going to a convalescence depot, be downgraded and given an easy job, not in front of all these other blokes. If I did, I would perhaps face a verbal onslaught from the sergeant and be shown up. So I said I was with the Royal West Kents, hoping to get a chance to sort it all out later, but I didn't. In a way though, I was glad to be back in India, feeling free and enjoying the respect I received from the locals. It was as if I had gone back in time a thousand years, bullock carts trundling along, high pitched music and singing wailing all around, a sacred cow chewing aimlessly. This was my type of life in the hot dusty climate, not like an ordinary soldier at home. Here people would rush to carry your bag, shine your shoes, sell you fruit and tea and it cost virtually nothing. Even the prospect of an uncertain future seemed part of the adventure. It was confusing really, you couldn't wait to get home and then you wanted the freedom and lifestyle we had out here. It was strange. Anyway, we were sent to Calcutta and then by boat across the Bay of Bengal to Rangoon to go back to the Burma front line. I had not been there before, as Rangoon had not long been taken back by our forces. There we were met by my old Signals Sergeant. He was in the Arakan, one of the old members of the West Kents, having served in the Middle East. I forget his name but he was at Kohima in the Signals Bunker just a few yards higher than our trench and had served in the front line throughout the months I had been away in hospital and home leave. He said it would be too risky to return to the company that night so we had a night on the town in Rangoon.

We took the opportunity to visit the sights. One such was the Swedagon Pagoda, a vast complex of statues and hundreds of Buddhas sitting and lying in small temples. It was night and as we soldiers wandered round as a group, we could see the priests in their saffron robes, their heads shaved, attending the candlelit shrines. I lit a candle and made my wish and gave the candle to a young Burmese woman with white flowers in her hair. With the thought of impending action, I wished to be home again. After our visit to the pagoda we went to a Chinese restaurant for a meal of lobsters, large prawns, salad and coffee.

The next day our Sergeant drove us very fast out of Rangoon as there were Jap snipers about. We went along the tarmac main road, passing through the flooded paddyfields on either side, driving through the monsoon rain, only broken by short hot periods of sunshine. As we travelled, we could see clusters of palm trees around villages, with people tending their water buffaloes. In the distance I could hear the faint sound of gunfire and began to tense up with that feeling of dread I had experienced before. I knew it would pass when I had got used to being in action again, but it didn't help at that time. We passed through the wayside villages, the huts were on stilts, one even with an open front selling fruit, amazing sights. We arrived at BHQ, a tented site in a sea of watery mud. This was a gloomy place indeed and thankfully someone else had got my job as runner and I would return to my Company away from here. We took off for 'C' Company which was fortunately sited in another village with huts on stilts. I was allotted to a hut with some others, people I knew from the old days, but quite a number of new young lads. They filled me in on what was happening. They had been patrolling a twenty mile area to clear the Jap odds and sods, after the race to capture Rangoon in the past days. The main road was still unsafe to use and it was said that a lorry taking some soldiers back to Rangoon to catch a troopship to England had been ambushed, killing several of the men, just before I arrived. So now back in the platoon of 'C' Company, I would be joining one of these Jap clearing patrols. I only did a couple of sorties before we moved on.

We got transport to the area we were to patrol, cutting down on the marching we did in the previous campaigns, but still having to cross the flooded paddyfields. Some were now drying out, but others were flooded with streams flowing through them. We stored cigarettes and matches in our steel helmets as we waded across the streams of paddyfields and I pitied non-swimmers or very short people. The water was at least waist deep and rising slowly to over our chests and deeper. We passed the deepest point and climbed out the other side into the shallower water of the paddyfield. As we approached the villages on higher, drier ground, about a dozen water buffalo with their vast sweeping horns lowered their heads and turned towards us getting ready to charge. We continued to approach the village and our lives, or rather the lives of these buffaloes, depended on the ten year old Burmese lad who appeared to be in charge. He was armed with a catapult, firing clay stone marbles. The buffaloes began to form a half circle and started to move forward. We stood our ground, our rifles and automatic weapons ready to fire at about one hundred yards. The young lad in charge of the herd saw the danger and started shouting at the buffaloes, at the same time he sent a volley of clay marbles from his catapult at them to break up the charge. Fortunately it did, maybe saving the animals lives and perhaps the village food supply.

We moved forward and checked out the village for Japs. There didn't appear to be any and the villagers said that there were no Japs in the area of their village. So we carried on with our patrol, meeting up with the trucks at the pick-up point on the road and later returned to our base. A large clay vase lay on its side outside our hut. It was about four feet high. Seeing that it could store many gallons of rainwater for drinking and washing we placed it under the eaves of the thatched pitched roof of our hut and as the waves of the monsoon rain fell, the large vase soon filled to overflowing. We took full advantage and filled our water bottles, washed out our mess tins, or simply just washed down our bodies and had a shave. We were at the village for some days and I had noticed that some of the huts were empty, so I had a look round. In one I found a roughly made crossbow and repaired it with a piece of signal wire, used a six inch nail for a bolt and fired it at a tree trunk. The nail buried itself an inch into the trunk, making it difficult to retrieve. I messed around a little longer with my new found toy and went back to base.

Some days later 'O' (Operations) Group called and we were given a job to do, blocking the escape routes of several thousand Japs now trapped in the Pegu Yomas. They were dying of disease and starvation and getting ready to try to break out to get to the Siam border across a main road which was close to us. We were ordered to move towards Pegu and travelled by jeep train, the jeep drawing flat top trucks to a railway embankment, overlooking a track to the main road. We dug in on the embankment and could see across the flooded paddyfields, with the village in the background and one of the escape tracks the Japs might use to reach Siam, or remain to die in the low jungle covered hills of the Pegu

Yomas. It was our job as fighting patrols along this track, to bump into any leading groups of Japs that had started to move out from the main body. As we climbed into the flat top trucks I put on a new bush hat to protect me from the sun, but out among the paddyfields the wind was blowing and a gust of wind whipped it off my head, leaving me sitting on the truck watching, as it was blown far away across the paddyfields, lost and out of sight. So it was back to the steel helmet.

We lived in the open, in the rain and sunshine, day and night in our trenches, while we remained in our position to block these escape tracks between the paddyfields to and through the village a couple of hundred yards away. We were at company strength here, the platoon spread out with standing patrols already out in the village. We built our slit trenches up with higher parapets, but as we went down a couple of feet, they flooded with water. At the bottom of the built up railway embankment was a paddyfield, now flooded and full of weeds, water plants, fish and frogs. I was not happy with this position, as it would limit the use of grenades thrown at any attacking Japs moving out of the paddyfield water. Here, it was a battle for the Bren or rifle and bayonet, or other automatics, but we were told we could call on the support of air strikes, tanks and artillery at our rear, if required. I decided to take things a little further and put out pungies; small, short lengths of bamboo stakes in the two foot high grass. These were positioned at forty five degrees and stuck about six inches out of the ground, near our trench with trip wires hidden amongst the stakes. This was to try to stop any Japs surprising me in the night. If they did come they would trip and fall onto the pungies, giving me a chance to shoot first.

After two nights on guard we heard splashes in the water and a sudden silence of the croaking frogs. It was quiet for about five minutes. I strained my eyes; rifle and fixed bayonet ready to beat off any attack. The frogs started up again calling to their mates and we were safe again for the time being. This went on night after night. We stayed very much alert but no enemy came.

One day we were needed for a fighting patrol and a full platoon of twenty men, including me, were led out by an officer. Information had been received that a Gurkha patrol had trouble clashing with a large number of Japs that had retreated back down the track again. The Gurkhas had taken some wounded. It was thought the Japs would attempt a break-out here, so it was decided to send a fighting patrol from our Company to check it out. We moved out in single file, no talking, passing through the village, out in to the open countryside of the paddyfields which then quickly changed into six foot high marsh reeds or grass either side of the track. We were still alert and moved more slowly, our weapons at the ready. Sections spread out on either side of the track ready for action, but none came.

Later we heard shouting and crashing of many feet coming in our direction, but we couldn't see anything behind the high screen of reeds and marsh grass. On the left hand side of the track our officer signalled to us to halt and we spaced out and took up positions of all round defence. The enemy seemed to be just yards away, behind the reeds. We had our safety catches forward and were ready to fire. Then about ten yards in front of our officer, the leader of a large herd of cattle smashed down the tall reeds and high grass to cross the track, disappearing through the high grass. Behind were the rest of the herd with the drover still shouting at them in Burmese. They did not seem to notice us. We covered a further mile or so to open paddyfields and had come far enough, it was time to go back. We returned along the same track to base.

A day or two later we were detailed to take over from others to do a standing patrol, watching and listening, in our case to the dogs on the other side of the village. We were not sure if the dogs were just barking or whether a group of Japs were around in that part of the village, remembering how the dogs in the village used to bark at our soldiers when they went out on patrol. The dogs did stop barking and a village woman offered us some tea without milk or sugar in a saucer like bowl. We accepted thankfully and gave her some cigarettes, a change from the thick type of cigar that most old Burmese women seemed to smoke. Later we did a little trading, some fresh eggs for tins of sardines.

We remained in that defensive position for two weeks until some Indian troops took over and then we moved out. These new troops immediately placed two Vickers machine guns in the places where we had mounted two Brens. I thought that was just the weapon needed to wipe out thousands of Japs crossing the water logged paddyfields or coming down the track in force, as these could fire a thousand rounds before reloading, whereas the Bren gun magazine would have to be changed after thirty.

It was August 1945. We received news that the Americans had dropped atom bombs on Japan. We were returned to Rangoon after a few more patrols around the Pegu area. There was talk of gliders for attacking some coastal guns on part of the coast near Malaya, but some of us were given a job in Rangoon for a couple of weeks, looking after Japanese prisoners of war at the local jail. Mind you, we felt like prisoners ourselves locked in a wild west style courtyard with a lot of Japs, and iron bars all around. We were allowed to smoke and as you did you were watched by the Japs shuffling around, waiting for you to throw away the stub-end of your cigarette. Then the Jap would move forward and point to your cigarette end on the ground and hiss like a snake whilst standing to attention, bowing all the time until you gave him permission to take it up. I would let him pick it up and again he bowed and hissed until I waved him away. Some soldiers were not as soft as me and would simply put their foot on the cigarette and raise a rifle towards the prisoner and send him away with a volley of verbal abuse.

While I was there, I had to escort a Japanese NCO to the cookhouse. He spoke good English and had a sense of humour. We reached the cookhouse and suddenly his voice changed as he bellowed orders to the others, sounding like some wild animal. He was tall too, seeming like a giant amongst the smaller Japs as they rushed about to obey his orders, bringing some rice cakes to him. As he turned to me, his voice changed as he politely offered me some. They smelt good and I was embarrassed. But although I did not mind talking with him, there was no way I could share his food. He was still the enemy and our troops were still fighting them. Anyway I refused. He was quite upset, perhaps losing face in front of his men. But we were still at war. They were our enemies. You don't eat with your enemies, especially when I recalled the treatment they gave our wounded and prisoners at Kohima. Tying them to trees with barbed wire and bayonetting them, even after they had surrendered.

Off duty we would go and have a look round, have a meal or visit the local bazaar in the Chinese quarter. On our way back one time we heard small arms fire and thought the Japs had infiltrated into the town. Then we saw a jeep with some officers firing their pistols into the air. They were shouting and cheering that the war was over and the Japs had surrendered. When we got back to the jail we told the Japs the news. They got angry and shouted abuse, refusing to believe us. They were frightened now, worrying about what would happen to them.

The Japanese prisoners were well looked after and well fed and this was in contrast to our own soldiers that were captured. We saw them waiting for the boat home, thin and sick. They were in a dreadful state and were shocked to hear that the Japanese were so well looked after. They wanted to shoot the lot of them. We were always on edge guarding the prisoners. We had been fighting these people for months in the jungle and they were still our enemy even now.

Around Christmas 1945, we were detailed to oversee the local dock workers, or 'coolies' as we knew them. They were loading and unloading the boats at the harbour and it was our job to see that everything went where it was supposed to and none went missing. We were sometimes given a few of the damaged fruit tins but unfortunately on one occasion, I ate a dodgy tin of pears and caught tapeworm. I first noticed the end of it wriggling in the remainder of the fruit after I had just swallowed some and immediately threw the rest away onto the deck, crushing it with my boot. The MO was not that sympathetic and gave me a dressing down for not keeping the rest of the pear. He said that if I'd done so, he would have been able to identify the sex of the tapeworm, to see if it would breed inside me. I hadn't and so I was hospitalised for nearly two weeks, to clear my system.

Fortunately, the war was over. However, I had to remain as I had signed up until 1949 and our job continued. Soon after leaving hospital, I was detailed with others, to track down bandits whilst some semblance of order and discipline returned to the country. Although the job was still difficult, the pressure was not as great and during rest periods some of the men would fish in the ponds that the locals had behind their huts. Some chaps even had Burmese girlfriends and they weren't pleased at all when it was time to move on, preferring to stay rather than go home. It was now 1946 and my one month's home leave had come through, so I returned to England on a ship called the 'Stamford Victory', sailing to Southampton. Some days after leaving Gibraltar, a cool breeze blew in our faces as we stood on the gun deck looking out to sea. We were in our thick battledress now, on our way home. Someone pointed to some dark clouds on the horizon, shouting, 'There's England'. We all laughed, saying how can that be England, it was just clouds. 'You'll see,' he said. He was right, some hours later, Southampton was in plain view. As we approached, I had mixed feelings. Things were confusing and unreal after all that had happened, but as usual the army didn't give us time to think. The order came to parade and get ready to go ashore. Kit, kitbags and all other things had to be sorted out, but as soon as we got ashore we boarded the train for home.

After my leave, I returned to duty at Maidstone Barracks. After a few days I felt sick during dinner and threw my food away, only to be put on a charge by the NCO for wasting it. But it was too late for him to make it stick, as hours later I was in a military hospital with malaria. Ten days later I was a lot better and sent onto Kingston Convalescence Depot. Unfortunately though, after eating a bag of black cherries, I awakened a former dysentery germ from my jungle days and found myself with the worst type of dysentery, amoebic dysentery and was again hospitalised. Afterwards, I returned back to Kingston Camp for 'E' Board and was finally discharged from the army in 1947.

As I made that journey back home to Birmingham, I recalled some of the actions in the Arakan, Kohima and the Imphal road and remembered that a monument had been raised at Kohima to commemorate those poor chaps that died. The inscription at its base seemed very apt of our dead comrades:
"When you go home, tell them of us and say, for your Tomorrow, we gave our Today."

Well I think I have now!

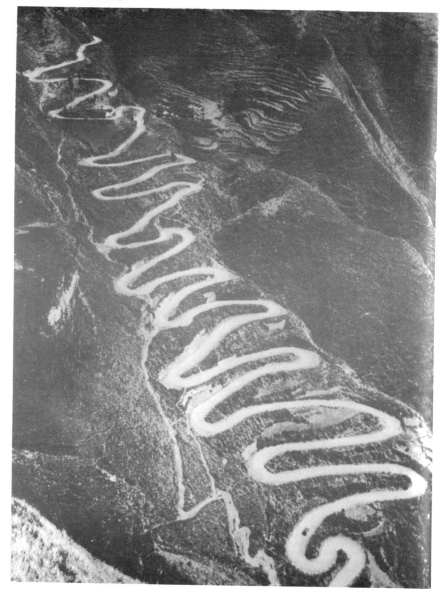

The Burma Road

A living bridge in the Burmese jungle

Japanese troops move through a sugar cane field

British troops

Allied troops entering Burma

RAF Thunderbolt fighters sweep over Burma

British 36th Division drive Southwards along the railway 'corridor' in Burma

Re-opening the Kohima-Imphal road

A British tank crosses a river north of Imphal

British soldiers crossing the Chindwin River

A Seaborne attack on the Arakan coast

*British soldiers ford the Nankye
Chaung*

Allied troops crossing the Mogaung river

The 14th Army clearing booby traps and burying the enemy dead

A mule convoy makes it's way up the Ngakyedauk Pass